EVERTONIANS
The Chosen Few

We are born,
we do not choose

EVERTONIANS
The Chosen Few

We are born,
we do not choose

Cliff Green

PUBLISHING

Contents

Foreword

The Everton fanzine "Speke from the Harbour" was conceived by the Northern Ireland Everton Supporters Club at the start of the 1990/9 season at the height of the fanzine movement, when the choice of match day reading was limited to the official club programme or the local 'pink' Football Echo.

The original editor handed over the reins to myself based in Liverpool only six issues in and, together with a small band of Blues, we worked together tirelessly on producing a magazine which aimed to provide a forum for the unexpurgated thoughts of Blues everywhere. Secondary to that ideal was the chance to try to put a smile on our readers' faces. We always tried to look at the lighter side of football whilst never missing an opportunity to poke fun at our nearest rivals.

In those days, long before commercially available word processors and slick desktop publishing software, it was not unusual to find me up to my ears in Pritt Stick cutting out pictures from the daily newspapers to include in the mag or 'typing up' an article on a typewriter. I even recall one or two hand written articles in those early days! It was a labour of love, especially when it came to selling the magazine in the notoriously unpredictable British weather.

After some 21 years and 117 editions the final issue was produced in April 2012 when the demand for instantaneous information and the advent of widespread internet forums and smart phones saw sales tailing off (and the sales force hitting middle age and having better things to do before the games than standing in the aforementioned inclement weather for 2 hours before the game i.e. going to the pub or having a chance to introduce Everton to the next generation, in my case my sons Robert and Daniel).

Cliff started writing for the magazine in 2004 and his unique style and perspective provided a refreshingly alternate interpretation from the point of view of somebody who had a good knowledge of both Everton and football in general which had not been overly tainted by the UK/Sky TV media machine. His upbeat, forthright and well-reasoned articles were always a joy to read and gave rise to many positive comments over the years with numerous readers describing his articles as 'always the first ones they looked for' in the magazine. The way in which Cliff interwove his own personal life out in Uganda with Everton Football Club's trajectory provided for both interesting and distinctive reading and quite often one felt transported overseas and able to imagine his struggles, especially in those early years, to do something as basic as finding out the result of a game from a different continent.

I am honoured to be asked to write this foreword for his book as Cliff has supported me over all these years by contributing so much to the magazine. I know that Evertonians will enjoy this book as it contains all Cliff's excellent articles written by a man who has royal blue blood coursing through his veins.

Mark Staniford – July 2013

Introduction

So, there he was, shuffling on to the pitch in his baggy jumper looking like a throwback to his previous incarnation as a bin man. The next moment slumped at his right hand post, disconsolate, distracted, as if he had just received some devastating news or perhaps an unwanted P45. He appeared to have no friends. At that point in time, any friends he may have had claim to were actually in the Goodison changing room listening to Colin Harvey trying to explain how we were going to turn around a 2–0 deficit at home to newly promoted Leeds Utd. It was the curtain raiser to the season that followed the glory and gloom of Italia 1990 a month earlier and 34,412 people were witnessing this bizarre half-time spectacle from the four sides of the hallowed home of Everton Football Club. However, there were some who did not have their eyes trained on the Park End penalty area at around 4 o'clock on that August afternoon. They were finding much more entertainment from the first edition of *Speke from the Harbour* which had been on sale outside Goodison Park that day. The early nineties was a time when the football fanzine was gaining traction in its rise to the peak of popularity that was to last for more than a decade before the internet came to save the trees and destroy hard copy literature. *Speke* was to be at the forefront of this revolution for the followers of Everton.

Neville Southall had many fine moments for the Blues but that one man demonstration between the posts on the opening day of the 1990–91 season was probably not one of them. We all shared his frustration that, in the space of three years, our club had degenerated from First Division champions to something approaching relegation candidates and big Nev, seeing so many of his mates from that earlier glorious era leave or decline, probably felt the pain more than most, but his half-time sulk didn't really do any of us any favours.

For me, I didn't ever see that first edition of *Speke*. I had begun a new era of my own and was coming up to my first anniversary of living in Kenya. Twenty-three years on, the fanzine has ceased to exist. The golden age of crafted articles written by the fans replaced by instant comments and throwaway lines on Twitter and Facebook by anybody with a vague interest and often little knowledge of the subject matter that they purport to have strong feelings about. My life as an Expat Evertonian has also ended and I now reside once again in the UK. The lifetime of *Speke from the Harbour* was almost exactly the same length as my life as a resident of foreign climes except lagging one year behind. A kind of parallel, slightly displaced existence 4,000 miles apart linked by a common passion.

Fast forward another decade from Everton's 3–2 opening day defeat at home to Leeds. We're entering injury time with the score 1–1 against West Ham at Goodison Park. Paul Gerrard, the Everton goalkeeper comes out of his area and gets injured. He's lying prone on the ground as the ball goes across the Everton box. With an open goal at his mercy, Paolo di Canio catches the ball. The ground falls momentarily silent and then 31,260 people give their spontaneous appreciation for an unprecedented act of sportsmanship. That's an exaggeration; the two thousand or so Hammers fans probably do not applaud and would rather have their erstwhile hero castrated for throwing away two unexpected bonus points. To this day, I am unconvinced that the chance was actually as simple as it may have looked. The ball came to the Italian at a difficult height and slightly behind him. It may have been an instinctive desire to preserve his imperious reputation in front of goal rather than an overwhelming altruistic chord in his heart that persuaded him to take this surprise course of action. Whatever the case, this apparent act of fair play made an awful match much more memorable than it should ever have been.

For a certain Violet Green it was going to be memorable whatever happened. She was my wife of four years by then and, having indoctrinated her into my football religion via satellite TV in Kampala, this was her first ever visit to Goodison Park. We were spending a rare Christmas in England and it just happened that outside the ground that day I bought my first ever edition of *Speke from the Harbour*. And so my association with the fanzine was cemented with issue No 41.

I immediately subscribed to have the fanzine sent over to Kampala and thus provide me with a much needed two monthly injection of humour and entertainment; a sanctuary from the slings and arrows of outrageous fortune that rained down on me daily as the Headmaster of Rainbow International School. The written word of its talented band of contributors allowed *Speke* to bring a familiarity and comfort to my life and cocoon me from the more troublesome aspects of expat life.

It was the summer of 2004 and Rooney's painful separation from his boyhood club that, not only prompted me to try to contact a Ugandan millionaire to salvage our ailing club (as explained in Chapter 24 of *Expat Evertonian)*, but also moved me to submit an article with a message of hope to the *Speke* readership entitled "The whole is greater than the sum of its parts". I was flattered, surprised and excited when the editor, Mark Staniford, said that it would be published in Issue No 66. And so my writing career on the subject dearest to my heart, Everton Football Club, was born. Many more articles followed over the next 7 and half years. Like that first article full of hope when many despaired at the departure of Rooney, I generally took a sanguine standpoint when discussing the affairs of my beloved club. It probably irritated some readers that I was always so annoyingly positive. I think that many felt that I was in a privileged position as I could watch every single Everton match usually live and always in its entirety without having to spend oceans of time and buckets of money like 'real' fans do. Instead I could view the satellite broadcast from my living room on the Equator or a local bar where the sun would shine all year round and the beer was just 50p a pint. And, therefore, I qualified as an 'unreal' fan. I understand their ire.

It did, however, allow me to take a somewhat detached and alternative perspective on Everton and the British football scene in general. As well as being infuriatingly upbeat, my articles were, therefore, often out of step with the hot topics of conversation around Goodison. Some were just quirky analyses of our current form while others were a general observation of the state of the game almost remote from Everton in particular although a tenuous link was invariably found. A majority were a thesis on how Everton were going to break into the big time as they have threatened to do for much of the past eleven years under David Moyes. In keeping with any self-respecting fanzine scribe, though, the logic of every argument presented is outrageously biased towards my own club. If my status as an 'unreal' fan has rested uncomfortably with many fellow Blues, I hope it doesn›t diminish their enjoyment of this book. Having shared my articles with fans of other clubs over the years, I do know that my opinions often chimed with much of the football fraternity outside of Chelsea, Man Utd and Liverpool. If you are a fan of one of those three clubs, look away now; otherwise enjoy the 'unreal world' of this particular football fan and you may just start to understand why followers of our great club believe that Evertonians are born; we do not choose!

Chapter 1: The whole is greater than the sum of its parts.

(SEPTEMBER 2004).

So, the painful departure of the prodigious Wayne Rooney was the event that finally compelled me to put into writing some of the hundreds of thousands of thoughts that filled my head on a daily basis about Everton Football Club. Being in Uganda, I was living in a football obsessed country but, sadly, most of the football adoring population at that time saved their devotion for the global brands of Manchester Utd, Arsenal and Liverpool. I was fighting a lone battle and the burning desire to share my views with like-minded people is easily understood. Sometimes preaching to the converted provides great solace when your day-to-day existence is testing; sending that first article to *Speke* was a cathartic exercise. As Headmaster of Rainbow International School, pulling such a large educational institution out of the financial mire had been a challenge. By 2004, I had largely succeeded as I had persuaded new owners to part with over a million dollars to purchase it in 2003. While I had hardly entered a stress-free zone, I could relax a little and divert my attention to the financial woes of my beloved football club instead. And at the beginning of the 2004–2005 season, we had severe woes; it seemed that the sale of the precocious Wayne Rooney to Manchester Utd had saved us. While his apparent betrayal was causing many Evertonians heartache and anger, I chose to interpret transfer deadline day in August 2004 as a turning point in the history of Everton Football Club but not a turning point downwards. Rooney hadn't played a game for us that season, having been injured at the Euros in Portugal, and he had apparently just completed his transfer when Everton, relegation certainties in many eyes, went to Old Trafford on 30 August for a Bank Holiday fixture that every sane Evertonian knew we would lose. We didn't. We drew 0–0 and that seed of hope was the kernel of my debut entry in *Speke from the Harbour*:

"I'm the Headmaster of an International School in Uganda; a beautiful country and a beautiful school. In many ways we are behind the times here and, as you would expect, much of the population is uneducated and backward. Much of the population support Man Utd. I don't believe those two sentences are unconnected. Inevitably, at the start of this academic year, many of my students have been keen to remind me that Rooney has become a red (or, going by his press conference, has always been a red, secretly). My retort to these taunts is that, on the evidence of Monday's match (0–0 at Old Trafford) "you need him more than we do". Of course, we all know that that is not true but, what the hell! I'm the Headmaster and so there must be some wisdom in what I say. The bemused Man Utd supporting students fade away wondering exactly what their Headmaster is trying to say. Behind the scenes the reality cuts deep. My traumatised seven-year-old son, so proudly wearing his blue Rooney shirt since his sixth birthday, now wants to erase that awful name from its back. A few weeks ago he said to me, "Dad, I know why we hate Liverpool, but why do we hate Man Utd?" Now, he needs no answer. But that is where a glimmer of hope emerges from the emotional debris. My seven-year-old son, with no instruction from me, has not even begun to contemplate following Rooney down the M62. Remember, this is not a young boy who has been brought up on Merseyside drenched in the blue blood of generations of Evertonians that have taken him to Goodison Park since he could walk. In fact, apart from one pre-season friendly against Bologna last year, he has never seen the Blues in the flesh. In a way, Everton is just a name that he has plucked out of the air, albeit with a little guidance from his father. His younger brother is showing serious signs of becoming an Arsenal fan. Rooney was an obvious hero for an impressionable young lad to connect with; fearless, skilful and allegedly devoted to the team that he grew up supporting. Everton and Rooney were a perfect fit for our Christopher as a team and a player to idolise. Now that the player has departed, you would think that the easy option for a seven-year-old would be to follow that player wherever he goes. But, no; all Christopher wants to do is keep the blue shirt but somehow obliterate the name Rooney from between the shoulders. The shirt lives on, the player is history. In short, the club is infinitely more important than any individual.

When the future looks bleak, we often turn to the past for both solace and inspiration. We recall better days to see if we can find morsels of hope from the details of our cobwebbed annals. Inevitably, for Evertonians, the historical era of salvation to which we refer are those halcyon days of the 1984–1985 season before, of course, Wayne, whatever he's called, was even on this planet. Looking to the years leading up to Everton's most successful season ever, we find some little chinks of encouragement. At the end of the 1982–1983 season Steve McMahon left us to join Aston Villa. McMahon was another of those phoney 'true blues'. A ball boy at Goodison, a fan since birth etc etc. He broke into the first team in 1980 at 17 years old and was talked about as the best home-grown talent Everton had produced for many years. Was this the beginning of the end of Everton's long tunnel of gloom that was the 70s? Well, when McMahon left in 1983 saying he wanted to play for a successful team, it looked like another false dawn. How could he leave so early in his career especially as we had the brightest young manager in the top division (plucked, incidentally, from a North West team in the division below) who was putting together a team for the future? Couldn't he just be patient? OK, so Villa had recently won the league and the European Cup and were playing in European competition every year and Everton were stuck in mid-table mediocrity, but couldn't he stay and help his beloved Blues to improve? It seemed not and many of the Goodison faithful were angry and disillusioned. Sounds familiar? In the next four years Everton won every domestic trophy available apart from the League Cup which we lost in a replayed final against Liverpool. We also won the European Cup Winners Cup and would have gone on to dominate Europe but for the shocking behaviour of Liverpool fans at Heysel. Meanwhile Villa were relegated. Not with McMahon, of course, as he had compounded his ignominy in the eyes of Evertonians by joining Liverpool. Such betrayal, and just like that arrogant kid who's just left us for United – can't remember his name – it seems McMahon was a closet red all along, just a different red.

More crucially in this time of need, though, when Evertonians are looking for any sliver of hope moving forward, that Everton team of the mid-eighties was 'the team of no stars'. There was no room for an eighteen-year-old overblown ego in the team. All the superstars of that time were at other clubs; Dalglish at Liverpool, Hoddle at Spurs, Bryan Robson at Man Utd and so on. Individually Everton couldn't compete but, as a team, we could beat anyone in Europe. Times have moved on I know. Money has dictated that some clubs can literally assemble a squad of absolute international superstars and any success-ful team nowadays probably needs at least two or three 'big names'.

However, when watching a recording of our 0–0 draw at Old Traf-ford until 2.30 am (it was a working day here in Uganda, so I missed it live) I felt a growing sense of pride as the game progressed. Man Utd might say that they were missing Keane and Van Nistelrooy but they did have the referee on their side and we were missing Gravesen and Yobo which, proportionately, is the equivalent loss for Everton. I saw players like Carsley, Stubbs and Hibbert making up the gulf in class with team spirit and a sense of passion for the blue shirt. The team was clearly much greater than the sum of its parts. I also saw a small right, wide player*, upright and balanced (remember Trevor Steven?) and a dominant, reassuring goalkeeper at the back. (Remind you of someone?) For those that question Eriksson's judgment as England's manager, and who doesn't, the conclusive argument must surely be the fact that Nigel Martyn was overlooked for the Euros. It's a shame that Martyn, Ferguson, Stubbs, Campbell and Weir aren't all ten years younger but, with the exception of Campbell, they can surely hang around long enough for a group of youngsters to be bought or brought through the ranks to join Osman, Kilbane, McFadden, Cahill, Yobo and Hibbert to form a decent side.

Clearly money is the unknown factor and it seems that the deal we negotiated with Man Utd for that fat overrated teenager (whatever he's called) was designed to accommodate Man Utd's cashflow requirements far more than Everton's, but there is hope and there are parallels with that golden age of 20 years ago.

Oh, yes, and when was the last time that we lost 4–1 at home to a team from north London on the first day of the season? That's right 1984... Now, that is being ridiculous. But that is how we Evertonians survive, isn't it?"

*Leon Osman.

As it turned out, this proved to be quite a prophetic article as Everton's 'team of no stars' qualified for the Champions League that season. Emboldened by what turned out to be such well-founded optimism, a theme for all future articles had been established. Supporting Everton is inherently coloured by disappointment and misery; my articles were to provide some grudging positivity.

Chapter 2: David Moyes; a man ahead of his time?

(NOVEMBER 2004).

The front page of issue number 68 of *Speke from the Harbour* featured a picture of our red-headed manager with the caption from the tagline of a famous telecommunications company "THE FUTURE'S BRIGHT, THE FUTURE'S ORANGE." Of course, I had no idea that that would be the cover picture when I submitted my article, but it fitted in well. With all Evertonians overwhelmed by our astonishing start to the post-Rooney era, the faith in our youthful manager, largely dissipated during the previous dismal season, was now flooding back. This was my attempt to examine what his X-Factor might be:

"I am becoming increasingly concerned with the expanding influence of foreign players and managers in the Premier League. Now, don't get me wrong, I'm not against foreigners per se; I am not a UKIP voter. In fact, I am undecided on the topic of how much Britain should integrate into the EU and I am waiting to be convinced one way or the other by listening to lucid, well-reasoned and honest debate on the matter from our politicians. Okay, so I will remain uninformed and undecided on that subject but, being much more passionate about and having much more knowledge of the beautiful game, I am infinitely more clear-sighted on the potential pitfalls of further foreign infiltration into our national sport. I am presently into my fifteenth consecutive year of living outside the UK and now I am in the position of running an international school in the heart of East Africa with 48 different nationalities on the roll. I can hardly, therefore, be a person who

practises or preaches xenophobia. I love my home country and look forward to returning there soon but, during my travels, I have learnt to embrace many different cultures and tolerate many characteristics unique to particular nationalities which has probably helped me to understand and accept more readily the idiosyncrasies of the British psyche. You only fully appreciate the mindset of your own people when you can contrast it with the mindset of others.

In most cases I am very accepting of alien cultures but, in the case of football in the UK, my tolerance has reached saturation point. So, what has prompted this concern?

Initially it was triggered by our defeat at home to Spurs on 2 October. As all astute Evertonians will have noticed, our only three reversals this season have come in the only three games when David Moyes was confronted with the tactics of a foreign coach. Sour grapes, maybe, would explain why I was developing this sudden attack of rabid jingoism. But I am not that shallow, am I? I decided to delve deeper to try to find an explanation for my feelings that was more rational than me merely being a lousy loser. Here is my theory:

After Arsenal had won the league last season playing football from a different planet, Sky Sports asked all the Premier League managers to give their verdict on the way they viewed Arsene Wenger's management style. As you would expect the praise was gushing and, almost without exception, the sentiment was that Arsene Wenger is the example that everyone should follow. I didn't hear what Alex Ferguson had to say (it was probably not broadcastable) but, from the interviews that I did hear, David Moyes was the only one who harboured any reservations at all. He was indeed complimentary of the Arsenal manager but then added something to the effect that Arsene Wenger uses methods and techniques that 'work at the moment'. At the time I was slightly dismayed by this comment; Arsene Wenger had coached his 'Invincibles' into playing futuristic football that, not only brings great entertainment, but also a bucketful of points and trophies. David Moyes, on the other hand, was presiding over a team that had just lost its last four matches of the season and was playing a brand of football that probably belonged in the Coca Cola/Nationwide League. I had just started to doubt David Moyes' managerial ability for the first time and had begun to question why players such as Gravesen, Rooney and McFadden all seemed to play better for their national teams under the tutelage of a foreign coach than when under the guidance of the Everton manager. I'm aware of the argument that they are surrounded by better quality players when on international duty, although does that really apply to McFadden? So, this view of Wenger from Moyes seemed ill-advised and started to cement a viewpoint developing in my head that David Moyes, so devastatingly effective initially through raw enthusiasm, was now showing alarming limitations in the areas of modern ideas and progressive thinking. The honeymoon was well and truly over and reality was setting in.

The manner in which the early weeks of this season have unfolded has forced me to re-examine these thoughts. Any manager who can keep a threadbare squad of such mediocre talent as ours in the top three until the end of October has to be listened to very seriously. So I revisited that Sky interview from the close season. When Moyes referred to Wenger doing things 'right at the moment' he was, perhaps demonstrating a vision that is too far in the distance for the rest of us mere mortals to comprehend. He was actually looking at the way things may eventually turn out in ten or twenty years time after the fantasy football of the present Arsenal team has run its course. I probably shouldn't keep mentioning Arsenal. They are an exception and in most senses do not fit in with the rest of this theory. Arsene Wenger, unlike other foreign coaches that have plied their trade in our top division, has actually spent a long time making sure that Arsenal were essentially British in temperament and style. How long did he continue with that ageing back five of Seaman, Dixon, Winterburn, Adams and Keown? And isn't Pat Rice still his right hand man? What Wenger has successfully managed to do is to superimpose over a period of time the flair and flamboyance of the continental player onto the British template of organisation and discipline.

No, let's leave Arsenal out of this argument; the league table shows that they are beyond comparison at the moment.

I believe that what Moyes was referring to and what he passionately believes himself is that the British public at the end of the day demand a British style of football. Continental managers have come but not lasted; for example Gullit, Tigana and Vialli. Even the Liverpool fans finally tired of the dross served up by Houllier. These people tried to bring continental football to these shores but all ultimately failed. Gullit and Vialli, of course, started an experiment at Chelsea that has continued through Ranieri and now Mourinho, but Chelsea are just slow learners; I'll return to their case later.

It first came to my notice in the 1990 World Cup Finals that international football coaches had acquired an obsession with possession. Keeping the ball was infinitely more important than taking a risk in the final third of the pitch to try to score a goal. (FIFA were so alarmed by this development that they changed the rule on goalkeepers being allowed to pick up back passes). In the 2002 World Cup Finals the situation had reached ridiculous levels when South Korea were 1–0 down to Germany in the semi-final and, with virtually everyone in the stadium and the entire country willing them to equalise, the Koreans were still playing keepball on the half way line with ten minutes of the game remaining. Gus Hiddinck had instilled such a rigid mentality in his players that they were unable to throw off the shackles even when a quarter of the world's population were imploring them to be daring, just once!

The day after our 1–0 defeat at home to Spurs, the point was brought home to me when two matches were shown on television back to back here in Uganda. Firstly Chelsea V Liverpool was like a chess match but without the excitement! I woke up in time to watch a brilliant 90 minutes of end to end action in the form of Birmingham City V Newcastle Utd. The match between allegedly the best coaches of Portugal and Spain may have been technically superior but was soporific whereas Steve Bruce V Graeme Souness may have served up pretty Neanderthal fare but it was one hundred times more watchable. The contrast was blinding. How long will fans of Chelsea put up with it? Like the Emperor's New Clothes, they may eventually realise that they are not really watching anything of substance after all. They may finally cotton on to the fact that hanging on to 1–0 leads when you have £150 million worth of talent at your disposal does not represent value for money and that Jose is just instigating an elaborate con of immense proportions convincing his followers to part with £50 for the privilege of experiencing mind-numbing torpor on a Saturday afternoon. I wonder how long it will be before England fans finally come to their senses and reach the same conclusion about Eriksson with his £4 million salary? Mind you, intelligent Chelsea fans (if that isn't a contradiction in terms) must have begun to question long ago just who they are supporting; a collection of mercenaries who happen to have assembled in West London because a Russian billionaire with dubious connections decided to buy their club.

So, back to the thrust of this article. Against Spurs, Everton tried to play fast, exciting British style football. We came up against Jacques Santini who, even if he hasn't assembled the necessary individuals to carry it out effectively, still enforces 'possession at all costs' football. Everton became frustrated and when Redknapp kicked Cahill off the pitch (was that also part of Santini's game plan?) and Defoe tried to do the same to Weir, the boring Londoners gained the psychological advantage. Everton grew tired of banging their heads against a brick wall and the game died as a spectacle; 1–0 to dull French pragmatism over exuberant Scottish naivety. But, is it naivety?

History has many examples of the cyclical movement of fashions and trends and of oppressed masses rising up to challenge the direction of change in order to rebalance things to something more palatable than that that their leaders wish to impose. It seems that Man Utd supporters are already sensing the impending danger represented by the American take-over of their club going by the rumblings being heard down Sir Matt Busby Way. It's not xenophobia, more isolationism; not wanting foreign infiltration of a British preserve; like MacDonalds buying up the local chippy.

In the 70s and 80s the 'English style' of football dominated its more sophisticated European counterpart (unfortunately Liverpool were the main protagonists in this phenomenon) but who's to say that the fast, passionate variety of football will not one day once again prevail over the more prosaic and precise version of the game? The British public demand it even if, at the moment, some are willing (or maybe are being force fed) the European flavour.

So, perhaps David Moyes is a visionary after all and, in a decade's time Chelsea, Liverpool and Spurs will have dispelled the continental myth and reverted back to having a British manager with a largely British squad. Meanwhile Eriksson will have been banished to Sweden after boring our nation with his sterile brand of football. And while Chelsea, Liverpool, Spurs and others are trying to rediscover the art of exhilarating, spectator friendly football, they will all be playing catch-up to David Moyes who saw all this coming years ago and started assembling his squad of world class, predominantly British players in the transfer window of January 2005.

I'm still undecided about further EU integration and how far to push the concept of 'The Global Village' but, when it comes to Everton Football Club, I know exactly what I want our identity to be and I think David Moyes thinks the same."

Eight years after this piece was published, Harry Redknapp was on *Match of the Day* saying how Everton was a 'real football club with 'real football people'. I wonder if, in a more obscure way, he was expressing the point that was being made in this article.

Chapter 3: Invisible Club.

(JANUARY 2005).

The media has immense power in determining public opinion. This is never more so than in the case of professional football, especially when that media is broadcasting English Premier League material to less informed parts of the world such as Sub-Saharan Africa. As we entered the New Year of 2005, Everton were still holding their own in the top four. The media, both in the UK and in Uganda, seemed to treat our infiltration into the higher echelons as an aberration; that our points total had somehow been added up incorrectly. Man Utd, Chelsea and Arsenal continued to dominate all football conversations; Everton's presence in that exalted company was not derided, not cynically chuckled at, but was simply ignored. Like a fly on a television screen, The name 'Everton' in the top four of the Premier League was a subliminal irritation hardly consciously digested, may be even vaguely annoying but soon to disappear. Certainly not worthy of mention.

> **"I don't want to sound too much like a Headmaster, although that is what I happen to be, but I have to say that I am concerned with the direction that much of our youth are taking. I should also point out that I am not your typical Headmaster. Rather than philosophical sermons or sanctimonious lectures, my assemblies are littered with football analogies and references to David Beckham's lack of intellect. In addition I have introduced a new school motto, 'Nil satis nisi optimum' and I drive my Pajero around Kampala with the only custom made tyre cover in Uganda proclaiming that Everton F.C. are the 'Pride of Merseyside'.**
>
> **My concern, though, is with the infatuation that so many of our students have with Manchester United Football Club. Worryingly, there is**

also a bandwagon rapidly loading up with Chelsea FC written all over it full of misguided individuals attracted to the huge wads of money and the arrogance that inevitably accompanies such affluence. As yet, it hasn't yet reached the frightening proportions of the Man U juggernaut but the portents are grim. Liverpool support is in decline but the slope is nowhere near steep enough for the good of this beautiful country.

Inevitably many young minds are easily influenced by the aroma of success and they just have to look at the top end of the league table to make their decision as to which particular team to support. However, raising this argument above that of mere football partisanship, there is definitely a disturbing undertone to this whole issue. Everton have been near the top all season but none of our kids seem to have been tempted to adopt these gatecrashers from Merseyside as their team of choice. Again, not meaning to sound too much like a pompous old git but, as an educationalist, I am concerned with the role models that young people follow these days and their motivation for making such choices. Increasingly it seems that youngsters are attracted to idols that possess a combination of huge quantities of dosh, an almost obsessive desire to cheat authority and a very limited IQ. Let's take each of these characteristics in turn.

Amongst the Ugandan populace, it is easy to understand the fascination with money mainly because, for a vast majority, large amounts of it are simply unattainable. At our school, however, we are talking about rich kids with rich parents; diplomats' daughters, sons of royalty and the like. It seems that boundless riches merely breed an insatiable appetite for more and near contempt for those who possess much less. The worth of a person correlates directly with the size of their wallet. Not all of our students are of that disposition and not all are quite so wealthy although, taken as a whole with the indigenous population, they are generally in the top 10% income bracket. When it comes to supporting a football club, though, this base mentality comes to the fore. "Why should Rooney stay at a little club like Everton when he'll do much better at a big club like Man U and, anyway, Everton should be grateful for the money", was a typical utterance heard from our students last August when Rooney took the road to hell. Quite apart from the historical inaccuracy of this statement (in terms of tradition and longevity in the top flight we all know Everton is the biggest club of all) the argument that, somehow Rooney would become a better player and better person by mingling with the unclean rich of Manchester and earning more money than his limited brain could begin to calculate is fundamentally flawed and, quite frankly, galling.

The second apparent criterion for the ideal modern role model is to have an obsessional need to get one over on authority by cheating. Once again I will reiterate that I am not one of those "I come from a different planet to your average teenager" types of Headmaster. I went through my teenage angst phase; *Never mind the bollocks* and all that. It hasn't completely left me and I enjoy the occasional punch-up on the football pitch although not in a school match perhaps! And I suspect I am chiming with most football fans of all ages in that respect. Wasn't the supercilious nonsense spoken about the Man Utd V Arsenal match of September 2003 completely at odds with the entertainment that most of us derived from watching it? Why can they have similar scraps in rugby matches and everyone just accepts that it is simply the inevitable result of a testosterone explosion that is bound to occur from time to time in such an intensified physical, adrenaline-charged situation? In football, though, the authorities have pushed such actions underground with disproportionate punishments e.g. Lee Hendrie suspended for three matches for pointing his frog eyes too close to the delicate dome of that psycho, Danny Mills. The result is that the more devious amongst our football elite resort to altogether much more subtle techniques. The kids, brainwashed by the sanitisation of our game, also suppress their natural instincts to smile at an all out brawl, but amidst their sanctimonious hand-wringing, they admire the more surreptitious cheat. Hence they find the thuggish antics of Duncan Ferguson akin to a scene from some outdated Western but admire with relish the surgical career-threatening strike of a Roy Keane or Van Nistelrooy as it reminds them of the economical violence of a modern day thriller that they are more in tune with. Similarly, when they see Van Nistelrooy or Rooney con a penalty out of the referee, it is seen as something to be revered and, more disturbingly, mimicked.

The final sine qua non for any self-respecting modern day icon, it seems, is to be fairly intellectually challenged. It's very hard, as a teacher, to persuade kids to work hard at school in order to succeed in the future, when they all witness the multi-millionaire England football captain struggling to rearrange the most simple words into meaningful sentences in response to questions from the press; hence my frequent but forlorn attempts to convince our student population that Beckham is the wrong God to worship. Disappointingly I have had the same lack of success in trying to discourage our youth to follow Rooney as well as the various rap singers that plague this planet. The longer I have been in the teaching profession and the higher I have climbed the career ladder, the more I have reluctantly come to realise that educating children in matters such as morality and a correct value system, is as important as teaching them the rudiments of, for example, mathematics and the English language. No longer an advocate of the Pink Floyd mantra *'we don't need no education'*, I have come to accept that, with the nuclear family so often disintegrating (and the problem is rampant in the international community), the administration of a school takes an increasingly more significant pastoral and surrogate parental role. I steer well away from preaching but separating right from wrong in a child's mind is now an obligation of every teacher, an obligation often neglected. Religion is kept out of the argument (that is why I cannot refer directly to Evertonianism in my assemblies) but common sense tells every adult, no matter what their culture, nationality, colour or religion, what is correct behaviour and what is not. Supporting Man Utd or Chelsea in itself is not wrong. The motivation for choosing such allegiances may well be.

In the end, though, this article is not meant to be an opportunity for me to whinge about my inability to put my young charges on the correct and moral path. I cannot expect to convert a whole school of 700 pupils to Evertonianism (although just one would be nice!) No, the real point of this essay is to convey exasperation at how little help I am receiving from elsewhere; namely the media. Whilst my staff and I try to educate our youngsters, the media tries to manipulate them. Not recognising it as manipulation (how many of our students have spoken directly to a journalist?) but recognising the words of teachers as education and, therefore, something to be challenged, our children generally give the media a much more accommodating ear than their teachers. The media has a far greater capacity to manoeuvre young minds in the way they wish. It is, therefore, disheartening that they do all they can to reinforce in young people all the negative traits associated with Man Utd and now Chelsea as listed above by portraying them as, somehow glamorous or, at the very least, not to be criticised. So Rooney's tantrums can be brushed aside, Ferdinand's selective memory when it comes to drug testing can be excused, Van Nistelrooy's penchant for maiming opponents can be conveniently overlooked as can Keane's admission that he deliberately tried to end a fellow professional's career. All these acts can be dismissed as minor blemishes because the egotistical perpetrators ply their trade with the media's beloved Man Utd and, of course, they are stinking rich. The way that reporters sycophantically hang on to every word that Darling Beckham says, (and there are precious few to hang on to) is an insult to our and their intelligence. Don't get me wrong; I am not meaning to mock the intellectually challenged, but I wouldn't allow anyone to leave my school with such a limited grasp of the English language, except perhaps some of the foreign language children who have not been given sufficient time to acquire the syntax and vocab. The fact that Beckham has been failed so miserably by the British education system is a cause for national embarrassment, not an opportunity for him to be exposed on a pedestal as some bumbling illiterate.

I have been battling with this anguish for more years than I can remember, (it probably shows from this article) but it has been compounded this season by a new phenomenon; the invisible team! For one glorious eight day period after they had beaten their city rivals, Liverpool, this invisible team were actually second in the Premier

League. Despite this indisputable, mathematically supported fact, all we heard from the media was how Man Utd were nine points adrift of Chelsea and how Arsenal had five points to make up on their London rivals. It was even mentioned, after their defeat to the invisible team, that Liverpool were now a massive sixteen points off the pace as if that was somehow relevant. Meanwhile, the invisible team hardly received a mention other than confident predictions from an assortment of 'experts' of how they were going to fold after Christmas. Fair enough, TV and radio pundits don't wish to make fools of themselves by anticipating anything but a monumental decline for the invisible team in the second half of the season but at least they could acknowledge our existence, at least recognise that we had gained 37 points on merit and, therefore, had three points more than Man Utd on merit. However, that would be to acknowledge a team that, with the exception of Big Dunc, have players that generally behave like fair sportsmen, do not surround the referee at every adverse decision, do not dive, do not gloat and, more importantly, perform in the knowledge that, should they indulge in any of these unpalatable activities, they have a modest, humble manager who will berate them for such behaviour and not support and encourage them in the dark arts as a certain knighted Premier League manager does with his unseemly shower every week. No, Everton (there, I gave them away) are not marketable. How can the media fraternity make news out of a club that relies on such dull virtues as a strong work ethic, team spirit and self-effacement as well as possessing that real tabloid taboo of impecuniosity. Most newspapers only feel comfortable with stories abundant in cheating, arrogant boasts and references to loads of money. The tragedy is that our youngsters lap it all up and perceive these ingredients as an essential part of football and, because football mirrors life for many of them, the basis for their entire value system in life. So, as we came into the New Year, the collective sigh of relief from all the media types throughout the UK could be heard here in Uganda, as their adorable Reds finally took their rightful place in the top three of the Premiership. At last they could refer to the top three of the Premier League as Chelsea, Arsenal and Man Utd and not actually be lying as they had been for half a season. They can now breathe easily, assured that that aberration in the league table had now been corrected and, hopefully, that that nasty little invisible team would disappear for good. They probably thought of us as some sort of pacemaker, as used in long distance running, leading Man Utd along for half the race and now about to run off the track, perhaps not even to finish the course, as the Red Devils romp home.

So, as we enter 2005, there are a few things that I wish for: I hope that the Glazers buy Man Utd and turn Old Trafford into a shopping precinct. I hope that the true source of Abramovich's fortune is uncovered and he is despatched to a Siberian salt mine for the rest of his days leaving Chelsea trying to sort out their massive wage bill with a handful of roubles. Most of all, though, and slightly more realistically, for the sake of our next generation and the well-being of our impressionable offspring, I pray that the unfashionable does the unthinkable and that irritating little invisible team is still in a Champions League spot come the middle of May."

And, as it turned out, that is exactly what happened. The Invisible Team limped over the line in fourth place and, after a minor scare when Liverpool fluked the Champions League in Istanbul and tried to muscle us out of the competition as holders, we took our place in the qualifying round in August 2005.

Chapter 4: Success so close.

(APRIL 2005).

As Champions League football came into touching distance, Evertonians were becoming reflective, excited and nostalgic of other great moments in our history. This article was a maelstrom of all these emotions as we bit our finger nails down to the bone and prayed for Liverpool to keep losing!

"Regrettably I was turned on to the beautiful game in 1970 when I was an eight-year-old. I was captivated by the mesmeric midfield passing of Ball, Kendall and Harvey as they threaded through opposition defences on our little black and white TV screen on the rare occasions that I was allowed to stay up until past 10 o'clock on a Saturday night to watch David Coleman present 'Match of the Day'. I was also enchanted a few months later by the ghosted figures on that same TV as Pele and Revelino effortlessly brushed aside hapless defenders at will as I rose at an unfamiliar hour every morning to watch highlights from the Mexico World Cup before I trudged off to school, my head swirling with the images of another continent and in a newly discovered Utopia called 'planet football'. Such sublime football was justly rewarded, of course, as Everton won the league and Brazil swept to their third Jules Rimet trophy.

So, what's with the adverb 'regrettably' at the start of this article? It's because that six months baptism into the world of football turned out to be a cruel illusion; an over glossy trailer of what the football product really had to offer. Like the travel agents' brochure promising pastel cottages on golden sands only to deliver unfinished buildings and pollution, the reality of football in the rest of the 70s bore no resemblance to what I had witnessed in the first half of the decade's first year. The pictures on our television had been hazy and monochrome, maybe they had actually been a recurring wet dream that never really happened at all. Certainly the Brazilian teams of Germany '74 and Argentina '78 seemed to have no genetic relationship with the Brazilian players of the Pele era. And Everton... well, what can you say about our beloved club during that miserable time? Perhaps the defining moment of those ten years of our history was when that advocate of robust football, Gordon Lee, won the battle of wills with the mercurial Duncan McKenzie and our enigmatic entertainer was banished to Chelsea. Our one spark of joy in a colourless decade snuffed out without a second thought for the feelings of the many who were crying out for entertainment. The glorious team of 1970 was disbanded much too quickly and we can only lament the ten years of barren decline. Two of the midfield Holy Trinity of the Championship winning side came back to resurrect 'The School of Science' during the 80s but, since then, the malaise has once again set in. But this article is not meant to be a lesson in the recent history of our great club (most of our learned readers know it inside out anyway). Instead it is intended to be a wider look at how that early introduction to the beautiful game for this particular Evertonian turned out to be nothing more than a wicked deception. A deception that sadly I have to continue to live with and cannot extricate myself from. Even a heroin addict has more chance of kicking his habit than I do of flicking the off switch in the middle of a televised Premier League match. The one redeeming feature, though, in this sorry scenario, is that it is my own beloved Everton, the club that got me into this mess in the first place, that holds the key to release me from the cynical deception that I am now a victim of.

It was in the 70s and 80s that football cynicism was invented; firstly by the nasty Leeds Utd team of Don Revie and taken on by Liverpool who always ensured that there was a Smith, Souness or Jimmy Case on their team sheet to soften up the opposition and pave the way for a succession of trophies. In fact, those wonderful 'ambassadors' of English football may have conquered Europe but they also introduced the concept of 'win at all costs' into our game. I remember just before a League Cup 'derby' in 1987 when Liverpool's manager, Dalglish and all his staff refused to give media interviews because 'the game was too important'. Meanwhile cameras and reporters flooded Bellefield to get an inside opinion from Colin Harvey, Peter Reid et al. Thankfully, for the good of football, Everton still won the game with a late Gary Stevens winner at Anfield. This was just a mild forewarning of the tactics that Alex Ferguson, Ince, Keane and Van Nistelrooy would indulge in, in the coming years and, now, rather disturbingly, Jose Mourinho. The continental penchant for psychological warfare before a ball has even been kicked, introduced to these shores by Arsene Wenger and learnt very quickly by his Man Utd counterpart, has now reached alarming proportions with Mourinho trying to talk his players and supporters into a frenzy and his opposition into submission before every game. Technically no rules are being broken and fining Chelsea the equivalent of half of Robben's weekly wage when the line that defines unsporting conduct is overstepped, is hardly going to scare Chelsea or Mourinho, anyway. It does make me wonder, though, whatever happened to that lovely refreshing sport that I so innocently fell in love with 35 years ago? Tactically as well, the fear of defeat has swallowed up the adventurous spirit of the top coaches. The chapter on risk taking has been ripped out of the coaching manuals. While Brazil in 1970 would try to pile five or six goals past a bemused opposition, Mourinho piles on defenders from the substitutes' bench as soon as Chelsea go 1–0 up. While Pele would dummy the goalie for fun and then laugh as he put the ball wide of the resulting open goal, Eidur Gudjohnsen would, no doubt, be condemned to the reserves if he dared show such extravagant crowd-pleasing antics at 'The Bridge'.

Times are changing and it would be naive to believe that we could ever go back to a more innocent time. That root of all evil, money, is a major factor. It's unequal distribution means that no longer can the likes of Watford, Southampton or QPR challenge for the title as they did in the 70s and 80s and no longer can the likes of Nottingham Forest win the European Cup twice in a row (or even once, for that matter). As fans we all have long entrenched views on the game. We all know that Nottingham Forest is a 'small club' despite the European Cups and we know Newcastle Utd is a 'big club' despite not winning anything of note for generations. We therefore, know that, historically, Everton are probably the biggest club of them all. However, in the current football landscape, we could be considered a 'small club' and what we could achieve this year by finishing fourth, could be put in the same category as those of Forest 25 years ago. And there lies my reason for hope. In a very different style David Moyes is doing exactly what Brian Clough did in his heyday. He's gathering a pretty small squad of pretty average players to play beyond themselves every week in an organised and disciplined team framework. Brian Clough was media savvy; he was sometimes humorous, sometimes outrageous, but there wasn't the cynical attempt to gain the psychological headstart by undermining a referee. Indeed, his attitude towards match officials was exemplary and never would you find any of his players even question a decision on the field of play. David Moyes had one notable aberration this season when he questioned Mike Riley's decision to send off James Beattie against Chelsea but quickly reversed that viewpoint and generally avoids making such comments or excuses for his team.

So, once again, I am left eternally grateful to Messrs Ball, Kendall and Harvey for convincing me of the right path to follow three and a half decades ago. If I had chosen Man Utd or Chelsea instead I would now be tossed around in a moral dilemma, trying to savour the successes of my team while reconciling the fact that the success is being achieved through dubious methods and masses of money. I could cope with supporting Arsenal, I suppose, but, in the end, Everton satisfy all my needs. I can feel proud of its wonderful tradition, preach my football religion from a moral high ground and remain stimulated by that constant, tantalising, tortuous sliver of belief that possibly, just maybe, if we dare to dream, success for this wonderful club is just around the next corner."

As false dawns go, this was a whopper and no one could have foreseen the calamitous start to the following season that was about to befall Everton, although the writing may just have been on the wall when we ended this season, having secured that coveted fourth place, with two defeats and ten goals conceded against Arsenal and Bolton.

Chapter 5: Jamie, your time has come.

(NOVEMBER 2005).

At the end of the 2011–2012 season Everton buggered up Man Utd's hopes of a 20th league title when they drew 4–4 at Old Trafford. What was even more remarkable than the result was this fat guy who turned up on the right wing for the visitors for the last few minutes. When I saw him come onto the pitch, I had to squint hard to work out who this apparent pub player was, and then I realised, it was James McFadden, balding and pot-bellied. How incongruous, how remarkable that we still salvaged that amazing draw with him on the pitch. Ten years earlier he had been hailed as the Scottish Wayne Rooney and for a short period we boasted the most promising English kid and Scottish kid in the same starting eleven. By 2005, McFadden still hadn't even approached his great promise. With Everton rooted to the bottom of the table, this article looked for salvation from the unlikely source of our Scottish wonderkid finally coming good. Clutching at straws? You bet it was.

"OK, so hands up if you're panicking. Admit it. Didn't you wake up in a cold sweat at 6 o'clock Monday morning fretting, not over your job, or even lack of a job, not because you thought you'd slept through your alarm, but because that Arca free-kick for Sunderland against Middlesbrough the afternoon before kept recurring in your dreams until it finally shattered your sleep leaving you staring at the ceiling in a numb silence, trying to focus on the reality that we really are bottom of the league. Then, in the haze of those minutes remaining before you know that you really do have to get up and face the day ahead, the statistics start to stack up in your head like skyscrapers, larger than life, distorted by the semi-consciousness of your mind: eight defeats

out of nine matches played this season, 10 out of 11 if you count the back end of last season, no goals at home in three league games, 5–1 down in the first leg of the UEFA Cup having already nose-dived out of the Champions League at the first hurdle. Did I say distorted? Perhaps not. These really are scary statistics. With Man City, Spurs and Chelsea next up, they are not likely to improve much in the next few weeks either.

So, is there a 'get out of jail card' this time? We all remember Wimbledon in 1994 and Coventry in 1998. I believe our marketing people have even turned them into DVDs. Surely the genre has been exhausted, though, and we are not looking at another sequel to *The Great Escape* in 2006. At least, if it does come down to that, West Brom at home on the final day does fill me with more optimism than either Wimbledon or Coventry did on those previous two last day cliffhangers.

But, no, I honestly do not believe that we will be relying on King Kevin (Campbell) to rescue us in May (albeit in an opposition shirt this time) or, indeed, that we will be depending on a dodgy penalty decision or an unscrupulous goalkeeper to negotiate us successfully through the final 90 minutes of the season. No, well before then I believe we will be at least half way up the table and probably about to win the FA Cup! There are three reasons for this absurd optimism.

1. EVERTON NEVER PANIC. Having supported the team for over 35 years and knowing our unrivalled history of staying in the top flight, I know that somehow, even it came down to the last day of the season (which it won't) Everton always survive. There is an inner belief that we will not go down. I won't fall into the trap that the Chelsea Academy (commonly known as West Ham Utd) fell into two seasons back by deluding ourselves with the mantra that 'we're too good to go down'. On the face of it, Everton must be too good to go down. We finished fourth last season and all the changes made to the squad in the close season while, hardly being sufficient to make a serious Champions League challenge, were moves that strengthened rather than weakened what we had before. But as Carrick, Defoe, Cole, Johnson and Co at the Chelsea (and Spurs) Academy proved, ability without a strong team and work ethic is not enough. With Moyes in charge, I cannot believe we can be relegated due to a lack of shared spirit. He rightly turned down the likes of Bellamy in the summer because he did not want one bad egg (or ego) to destroy the collective will of the rest of the squad. Our proud history demands that we adhere to certain principles. We try to play a 'School of Science' brand of football irrespective of our league position. Too much is made by ignorant commentators of how we like to play the long ball to Ferguson. In truth, Everton rarely resort to that base tactic until maybe the last 15 minutes or so of a game that we are chasing. We always try to play through the pitch. All the great Everton teams of the past have had a cultured player or two in its midfield such as Colin Harvey, Alan Ball, Howard Kendall, Trevor Steven or Kevin Sheedy. Even in the unsuccessful sides we found room for players such as Asa Hartford, John Collins and Olivier Dacourt. Now we have Arteta, Li Tie and Osman; subtle players although perhaps a little too delicate on occasions. The point is, though, we have a tradition and a history to uphold and, as such, we do not panic. It means that we end up going through some dire runs; I remember eight defeats in a row after Kendall resigned as manger for the second time in 1993 and a similar sequence just before Gordon Lee was sacked, and then there was that torturous first half of Walter Smith's first season and the desperate start to the 1994 campaign under Mike Walker when we needed fifteen games before we registered our first win. The reason for these dreadful sequences of results is that Everton get stuck in a style of playing that is supposed to live up to our great traditions but, if we don't have the required calibre of players to achieve it, the football looks awful and so do the results. We could cut our cloth according to our quality, but we don't. Instead, there is a stubborn refusal to compromise but, in the end, we always come through and we survive to fight another day in the top division and, very occasionally, we actually have the right quality of players and it turns into something beautiful as witnessed in 1970 and 1985. So, once again, I am sure that David Moyes will follow his predecessors, know his history and will adhere to the Everton traditions and his faith will be rewarded with an emergence from this present nightmare.

2. MOYES IS BUILDING FOR THE FUTURE. I hope I am not just looking through blue tinted spectacles but I believe that David Moyes has a great vision for Everton Football Club and, for all the criticism aimed at his chairman, at least Bill Kenwright has the sense to give his manager the time to fulfil that vision. Let's be honest now, last season was a bit of a fluke. We finished fourth with a negative goal difference; a quirky statistic never achieved before by any top four side and, let's be fair, many of those 1–0 wins could have gone the other way. Seeing the Wigan game last weekend, the first half was not at all dissimilar to, for example, the 1–0 wins against Southampton, Norwich or Fulham last season. Fortunately, more of such games swung our way than didn't, although our luck started to run out in the second half of the season as witnessed in our home games against Blackburn and Charlton. In the end, last season was probably three or four seasons ahead of where we should have progressed to by that stage. This season is just a natural correction. Given our resources and playing squad, we had no right to be anywhere near the likes of Chelsea, Man Utd or Arsenal, let alone above Liverpool. It probably helped to accelerate our long term progress as our flirtation with the Champions League gave us much needed funds to strengthen the squad in the summer but David Moyes, himself, must know that, for the next season or two, we should just be consolidating top half finishes and then nudging the UEFA Cup places while, all the time, building the squad with players that fit his very clearly defined profile i.e. big heart, small ego and generally early or mid-twenties in age. Wigan are doing OK at the moment filling their team with the likes of Henchoz and De Zeeuw, but they are short-term survival players. We all know that, in two seasons at the outside, Wigan Athletic will be back in the Coca Cola League. Wigan and their ilk have no long term strategy or vision. David Moyes is thinking further ahead and, while the Everton rollercoaster may move in mysterious ways, its underlying trajectory is upwards and it certainly does not include relegation somewhere along the way.

3. ENTER McFADDEN. The final reason to console Evertonians in this time of despair and to convince us all that things are not as bad as they seem, is the rationale that we football fans love to resort to when logic fails; superstition. If you are not convinced by the arguments put forward so far and, let's face it, our current league position does suggest that I may have redefined the meaning of the word 'optimist', then try this theory instead; the 11-year rule.

In 1983 Everton had an appalling start to the season. We had scored something like five goals at home by Christmas and Howard Kendall was, by all accounts, one game from the sack. In 1994 we had our worst start ever to a season; three points and no wins after 11 league matches and absolutely rock bottom. There were other similarities with the two seasons. In both cases we began the campaign in August with high expectations. In 1983 Kendall was aiming to build on his first two seasons in charge when we had finished seventh both times and in 1994 Mike Walker had arrived in January and salvaged our Premier League status (just) and was now aiming to move forward having already shown at Norwich that he was a promising manager. In the end he was sacked in November and Everton's season was revolutionised by Joe Royle and we finished mid-table and won the FA Cup, almost an identical story to the transformation of our club after Christmas 1983 when we went on to lift the FA Cup against Watford and amazingly climbed to seventh (again) in the league. Simple maths will tell you that 2005 is the next year in the 11-year cycle. Sure enough, we began with high hopes but, approaching October, we are in desperate need of some resuscitation. Interestingly the revivals in those two aforementioned seasons coincided with the arrival of a Scottish centre-forward in the autumn who galvanised the team. In 1983 it was Andy Gray, in 1994 it was Duncan Ferguson. In 2005 who can it be? With a transfer window now a feature of the calendar which it wasn't in those previous two cases, such a tartan Messiah cannot arrive via the transfer system at such an opportune moment. If we wait until January, it really will be too late. However, recalling the Wigan match from last Saturday, I saw a Scottish centre-forward in a blue shirt that I had never seen before. His name was James McFadden, but unlike the James McFadden that I had seen play for us before, this version actually controlled the ball instantly and held it up and passed it and dribbled it past people without running out of pitch or into the next defender. He even had the occasional shot that was vaguely in the direction of the goal.

So, in conclusion, if we are to follow the inexact science of football superstition, the outcome of this season should be blindingly obvious to all Evertonians. 2005–2006 is the season when Everton come back from the dead to finish half way up the league and win the FA Cup all inspired by the belated discovery of an exceptional Scottish talent by the name of James McFadden!"

Everton amazingly did finish the season in mid-table but all other predictions, including the expected early demise of Wigan, proved as wide of the mark as most of McFadden's attempts on goal.

Chapter 6: Keano nearly saved my life.

(FEBRUARY 2006).

As Everton continued to flounder through a bleak winter, it was becoming ever more difficult to find crumbs of consolation. Facetious remarks to Liverpool fans about their team's increasingly Iberian identity was about all that was left to entertain us after a miserable Christmas 'derby' defeat. That and some masochistic joy gleaned from the fact that a certain midfield thug did not join our ranks as had been suggested by the festive Premier League rumour mill.

"I'm writing this in the wake of our 3–1 defeat at home to Spain last night and, believe it or not, I am not too despondent. Some people may be getting tired of my persistent and ridiculous optimism but it's good to get some balance. We could all well be close to suicide otherwise. If the 'derby' game is broken down into key moments, things do not seem so gloomy. The stick insect (Peter Crouch) scored when Yobo went to sleep. Our hapless Nigerian number four then ducked out of the way of a Gerrard shot but not quite far enough, thus deflecting it past Nigel Martyn. Backwards Yobo spells 'O Boy' which is a more appropriate name for our normally accomplished central defender just at the moment. I know that it was a cold night but surely a highly paid professional footballer should have the courage to accept a smack in the face from an icy ball for the team's cause? A linesman then dramatically and unilaterally changed the rules of the game by deciding that the whole of the ball has to be *inside* the line for it to be in play, hence Beattie's header from Cahill's cross was disallowed. Beattie then scored a goal that the referee just couldn't

think of a reason to disallow. Back in the game, we prepared ourselves for a blue onslaught only for Cisse to find himself one-on-one with Weir. Knowing what an uncoordinated donkey Cisse is, Weir simply had to stand up and the ball would inevitably end up going for a goal-kick. Weir, however, failed in this elementary manoeuvre and we were 3–1 down. Graham Poll, who people have said has become more tolerant as he approaches retirement, then took over proceedings. Indeed, he was tolerant to Spain but showed not a nanometre of leeway (or brain power) in sending off Neville and Arteta. Even then, if Beattie had demonstrated, just once in his life, that he could aim a shot somewhere below the clouds we could have made it interesting at the end.

In summary I was encouraged by the following:

1. We were the first team to breach their defence in ten matches and would have done so more than once but for some very suspect officiating and Beattie's balloon shot.

2. After Phil Neville was sent off, you couldn't tell which team was a player down. Maybe this says more about Neville than Spain, though!

3. They had the worst player on the pitch (and probably the entire Premier League) in Sissoko and we had easily the best in Arteta.

4. If we could find a cure for this debilitating disease that has suddenly afflicted the limbs and brains of all our central defenders in the last four matches, Spain probably wouldn't have scored any of their three goals.

5. This so called new exciting version of our city rivals created across Stanley Park is actually a myth; they are still as uninspiring, metronomic and negative as all the other piles of dross turned out by the Anfield conveyor belt.

At the end of the day, though, the league table doesn't lie and we are still in a precarious position and this season has been one of the hardest of my 35 years as a dedicated Evertonian to endure. The injustice and frustration of the last three games alone have constituted 270 of the most difficult minutes of my football supporting career. Without the regular attacks of centre-half rigor mortis and some mysterious refereeing decisions, we probably wouldn't have lost any of the three games against Bolton, Villa and Spain. As it turned out, we lost all three and hammered our goal difference with a negative ten in the process. At the end of October we looked like relegation certainties. One month later we were secretly eying UEFA Cup qualification (admit it, you were, weren't you?) and now, as we end December, our thoughts have turned dramatically towards survival again. I'm 44 years old; as my old ticker becomes weaker, it seems my beloved football team is intent on inflicting ever more strain on it. So, there came a moment in mid-November when I thought that I had been presented with an escape route, a one way ticket out of the morass of relegation worries, a survival package to ensure a longer, more healthy life without the stress of hanging on to every football result. I could be a better father to my children, a better husband and altogether a much less angry and frustrated person. Perhaps I could even converse intelligibly with people not burdened by an interest in football and have weekends when I could surprise my wife with a romantic mini-break or be invited to dinner parties or treat the kids to days out at a theme park without worrying about kick-off time or the result or the depression that usually follows the result in the current climate. In short, I had a golden opportunity to exorcise football from my shallow existence, end my addiction and become a rounded, adult human being for the first time in my life.

This unexpected life changing opportunity came after our embarrassment at West Brom. (Now, there's a 0–4 that can't be rationalised by dodgy defending and eccentric refereeing). The result and performance hurt. If ever I needed a chance to be put out of my misery, it was then. As if by a miracle, it presented itself in the post match interviews.

I couldn't believe my ears or my good fortune. This really was the end of my Everton prison sentence; unexpected parole; early release on compassionate grounds. I would no longer be a danger to the public because my addiction had been cured. In his interview in the shadows of The Hawthornes, David Moyes hinted, simply by not answering the question, that he may be interested in signing Roy Keane. Everton, my beautiful football club, being associated with the biggest cheating thug that has ever set foot on a football pitch since Graeme Souness. The Antichrist that I have vilified and hated with every part of my body for the last decade and have broadcast that opinion to all and sundry throughout that time. This was a signing that I couldn't possibly justify to others or reconcile in my own mind. I could never support Everton ever again. I would have no choice but to release myself from this self-imposed exile from the normal human race. Roy Keane in a blue shirt? True, if he had played for us against Villa, Baros's basketball goal would not have counted and Marcus Bent's header would have stood. If he had played for us against Spain, Beattie's goal would have counted, Neville and Arteta would have remained on the pitch and Harry Kewell probably wouldn't have. When you have Keane in your side, you acquire a significant influence over key decisions as Man Utd have benefitted from for many seasons. That alone might be worth his place on the payroll to some people and some clubs but surely not for Evertonians and Everton. We love Duncan Ferguson when he terrifies opposition defences but we still want him to play within the laws of the game.

So, when a few weeks later, I heard the news that all law-abiding, upstanding football supporters in England could once again sleep safely at night in the knowledge that the Irish henchman had buggered off to Celtic, I suffered a strange paradox. On the one hand, Everton remained untarnished, still the True Blues dedicated to the principles of sportsmanship, upholders of fair play and phlegmatic acceptors of refereeing decisions good or bad. On a personal level, though, Keane's move north of the border meant that I was condemned to continue living with this terrifying, socially paralysing addiction with no legiti-

mate excuse to relieve myself of it. Also, equally disturbingly, I was, and still am, left with the unanswered question: Why on earth did Moyes even toy with the idea of signing Keane in the first place?"

It's a question many rabidly partisan supporters have asked when a previously hated individual is set to join their club. How can you reconcile an enemy in your ranks? In the end, we always cope; is it hypocrisy or just the fact that the club and the shirt are always more important than any individual? I still wonder if I could have ever accepted Roy Keane in an Everton shirt, though. Thankfully, my resolve was never tested.

Chapter 7: No way, Jose.

(MARCH 2006).

It seems that the wrath aimed at other clubs by partisan supporters correlates directly with the success of their own team. And it is a negative correlation, whereby the higher the success rate of your own team, the lower the level of vitriol directed at others mainly because, when you're winning, there seems less reason to expend destructive energy on others. When you're losing, sometimes the only consolation to be found is to hit out at others more successful. Have I just defined the term envy? 2005–2006 was a poor season for Everton and I was flailing around to find any target to project my ire towards. Having turned my anger on Roy Keane, next in the firing line was the Chelsea manager, Jose Mourinho. While housewives swooned and journalists fawned, this article homed in on the more sinister aspects of what the 'Special One' was doing to our beautiful game and to the careers of referees such as Anders Frisk.

"So, Peter Osgood died suddenly at a young age. Once again my mind is cast back to a golden era when my love affair with football began. I remember on a grainy black and white television seeing Osgood scoring in the 1970 FA Cup Final replay against Leeds Utd. The best World Cup Finals tournament ever was about to begin on the other side of the planet and I had just become inextricably attached to Everton Football Club and that wonderful championship winning side built around the Holy Trinity of Ball, Kendall and Harvey. Nobody hated Chelsea then. In fact, hate wasn't a word used so much in football in those days. If football reflects the times in which we live, then it is clear that the world is a significantly more polarised, competitive and money-obsessed place than it was thirty odd years ago. Chelsea prob-

ably epitomise recent human evolution more starkly than any other club. In 1970 they went into that Cup Final with the majority of the country's support firmly on their side as their opposition on that day was the uncompromising, unattractive and unloved Leeds Utd side of Billy Bremner and Don Revie. Chelsea had a style and a swagger that the neutrals could warm to. Last week they couldn't even boast the balance of the country's support when playing foreign opponents. Few tears were shed outside the Shed when Mourinho's men were out-classed by Barcelona.

I believe that Mourinho wrote in his programme notes for the FA Cup replay against Everton that he was unhappy about the lack of respect his team is receiving for all its achievements. I didn't see the article, so perhaps I shouldn't comment, but I will anyway. Knowing Mourinho's warped sense of humour, he, no doubt, wrote that article to encourage anger and vitriol from his enemies which account for virtually everyone in football who doesn't have a vested interest in Chelsea F.C. So, up to a point, I feel a bit of a mug writing this article being aware of the trap that I am falling into and the arrogant plea-sure that I will be affording Mourinho in doing so, if he ever came to read it. He, of course, will never come across this fanzine but I feel that someone has to express just how much 'The Special One' and his team are despised and why the actions of he and the Russian nerd have damaged football as a whole and the image of Chelsea in particular to the extent that Peter Osgood, God rest his soul, before his death, was probably embarrassed to be associated with the modern version of the club that he once graced.

So, here is a letter that I would like to send to the smug Chelsea supremo in response to his comments in the Everton programme:

'Dear Jose,

The reason that very few football observers, if any, respect your team is because it is a mirror reflection of your own character. It represents insincerity and cynicism to the nth degree. From the standpoint of being part of the football supporters' brotherhood, I have some sympathy with the Chelsea fans as they did not choose their leader. However, the fact that they have embraced this gold laden Russian revolution so completely has also made me realise that Abramovich knew exactly what a brainless, gullible congregation he was preying on when he identified Stamford Bridge as his plaything. Surely, no other section of the football fraternity could have been taken in so utterly by such a manipulative, money-mad regime. Even the pondlife that frequents the Stretford End demonstrated a semblance of self-respect, even principle, when they showed their dissatisfaction at the prospects of the Glazers infiltrating their empire. Mind you, if the Glazers had come with the kind of riches that the Russian geek brought to Chelsea, they may well have been a little less hostile. As with the population that believed in the Emperor's New Clothes, though, the Chelsea faithful will one day be made to look pretty stupid because, Jose, as you are fully aware, they are worshipping the wrong God. They may be football supporters but what they are supporting at the moment has little to do with football. As you know, you are in it for the money. You are not interested in Chelsea Football Club or its supporters. This is a business deal. You happen to have the right combination of coaching badges and charisma to land the top job at Chelsea. You couldn't actually care less whether you manage Chelsea or Cheltenham as long as you have £10 million a year in your bank account (or whatever you earn these days) and a huge number of adoring fans. Obviously you are more likely to get those things with Chelsea than Cheltenham, but it is just a job to you. Some might call it professionalism but, as with Eriksson and England, the calculated cynicism will eventually be exposed and even the most brainwashed supporter will have to concede that they were pretty naive to have bought it all. Sport is a unique business combining professionalism with passion. You have the former in bucketfuls but you possess precious little of the latter.

People are seeing through the facade, though. You may have thought you were clever enough to con everyone but soon only those pitiable Chelsea fans will be the ones still believing the vision you try to project. Your press conferences are an act, an almighty ego trip to see if you can say something even more outrageous and ridiculous than the last time to give yourself a slightly bigger headline or a few more column inches. Telling us that Barcelona have too many good players to choose from, for example, brought gasps from the media but only from those who thought you actually made that statement without irony. The comments about Arsene Wenger, Alex Ferguson, Barcelona, referees, opposition players, your own players and any other topic of conversation that might put you in the papers are meticulously prepared and stage managed to draw attention to yourself and massage your delicate ego. Some analysts have very charitably suggested that you do this to deflect attention from your own players thus keeping them relaxed away from the limelight. Charitable but, I suspect inaccurate. You are actually so aware that the more press attention you get, not only feeds your inflated self-image but also raises the value of your next contract. The need for a new contract may be closer than you think, as well, Jose, because you are running out of time. It seems to me that you are becoming so absorbed in your own self-importance that you will implode. You occasionally talk of your family values and putting life in perspective but you are actually thinking aloud, trying to convince yourself of those very values because, it appears, you lost sight of them a long time ago. Your big sulks with the press, spurious accusations against referees and bizarre allegations against Wenger are just some examples of your unstable state of mind. At the moment you are still being propped up by a phenomenal run of results but the signs are there and a few more Riverside-like debacles and you could well be heading down the river without the proverbial paddle to bring you back to mental equilibrium.

This probably sounds like the ranting of a bitter man motivated by the green-eyed monster. I have examined myself on this point. It is true that I was disappointed that my ambitious prediction in October that Everton would win the FA Cup this year was thwarted by you being in the luxurious position of being able to transform your team from the substitute's bench at Goodison to turn round a game that you should have been out of by half-time, while we could only try to cover up the cracks from ours. It's true that I am frustrated that you can buy complete garbage for stupid money like Jarosik and Tiago and not have to worry about the consequences whereas we pay £6 million for Beattie and have to keep selecting him until he looks vaguely worth the money. But this is anger at the injustice of the way of the modern football world, not jealousy. If it were jealousy, why would I continue to admire Arsenal and support them in Europe and against Man Utd, Liverpool and your odious shower, when they outdid everything that you achieved with two 'doubles' and an unbeaten season? Even when Arsenal hammered Everton 7–0, my sentiments were; 'it couldn't have happened to a better team'. No, Jose, I have no respect for you or your team because, like your pitch, you compete on an uneven playing surface and gloat over that fact. Not content with the £260 million losses you've been allowed to accumulate with impunity, you still constantly try to tip the balance further in your favour with your mind games and other dubious methods.

The Stamford Bridge cow field is a case in point. Knowing from last season that Barcelona were technically and tactically superior, you resorted to other means to reduce the gap between the two teams 'maintaining' the pitch in a condition the like of which, even Colchester from their humble background, had never experienced before. You then shamelessly tried to exert pressure on the referee before a ball was kicked (which spectacularly backfired, as it turned out). We can also talk about the way your club 'tapped up' Ashley Cole and used bulldozer methods to acquire the services of Kenyon and Arnesen and we can refer to your depressing coaching ideology that says that you must defend for the first 20 minutes of every match irrespective of the opposition and retreat into the same defensive shell as soon as you score. Worst of all, in my opinion, though is the gamesmanship that you instil into your players so that they feign injury to distract the referee whenever they commit a potential red card offence. Essien has survived on the pitch several times using that ploy. Del Horno must consider himself very unfortunate when he unsuccessfully tried the same tactic against Messi probably forgetting that he was up against a referee who had not been seduced or intimidated beforehand by your bullying methods or, indeed, your fans' death threats. The persistent attention-seeking antics of Crespo and Robben whenever they come within a meter of a physical challenge is not condemned by you, Jose. In fact it is encouraged by you, Jose. Why?

I can tell you, though, that the distaste with which the Chelsea brand is viewed is becoming universal. We were in the midst of presidential elections here in Uganda last week. It meant irrational and unnerving cheers could be heard around the capital, Kampala at the most unexpected times of the night and day as various rallies took place and politicians funded parties with free drink to bribe the electorate. On the night before election day, itself, there were two very distinct cheers that emanated from the bars around the capital city. They were not in response to another MP's handout but were for two goals scored by Barcelona at Stamford Bridge. For a country that idolises the English Premier League, that is quite a telling statement about the depth of Chelsea's unpopularity in this part of the world, as is the deafening silence in those same watering holes that greets any Chelsea goal scored. The Ugandan football public are not that discerning but they recognise boring football when they see it and they cannot forgive you for exaggerating Essien's injury to ensure that he did not participate in Africa's biggest tournament earlier this year. Soured by their own culture that dictates that success and power are entirely dependent on money rather than merit, they are dismayed to see that British football is being dominated by the same invidious set of values.

In summary, most true football fans wished for many years that the dire, dour dominance of Liverpool in the 70s and 80s and the money crazed monopoly of Man Utd in the 90s and noughties would eventually be overthrown. We did not realise that a club would come up with an even more toxic combination of both. A club that could trump both Liverpool and Man Utd on their worst traits. For the good of English football, we are all praying for a few more Chelsea humiliations like those encountered against Barca and Boro so that, by the time Everton, with their sincere and humble manager and honest and hardworking team visit Stamford Bridge on 17 April, Chelsea's Roman

Empire will be crumbling as the three points head back to Merseyside and Abramovich will be facing a peasants' revolt far greater than anything encountered by his bourgeois ancestors in 1917.

Glasnost has a lot to answer for!"'

Well, I got that off my chest! And while predictions of a rocky future for Chelsea have proved pretty accurate and Mourinho's reign was, indeed, relatively short-lived, Abramovich's methods have continued to reap reward, although he is now regarded much more as a figure of fun rather than an object of hate, as is his club. And, as this book goes to press, The Ego has landed again in West London. I give it 18 months, tops, before he's off again playing pantomime to the cameras of another nation.

Chapter 8: A team of two halves.

(APRIL 2006)

Everton's dire season was almost at an end. All my venom had been expended on Keane and Mourinho and I was left to ruminate over some strange statistical quirks of the previous two seasons.

"I gained a degree from the University of Liverpool 23 years ago in mathematical statistics. Many people have said that I have never got over it. Certainly my obsession with numbers concerning Everton Football Club has never diminished. I remember sitting in my first set of professional accountancy exams two years after graduating. Having just spent a week AWOL in Rotterdam watching us win the Cup Winners Cup Final against Rapid Vienna and then straight to London to watch us miss out on the treble in an FA Cup Final decided by a pearler from Norman Whiteside, I was ill-prepared for the rigours of 15 hours of accountancy exams crammed into 2 and a half days. The law paper, in particular, was a bit of a non-starter for me. I, therefore, had to somehow occupy myself for three hours in the exam room knowing that the prospects of actually writing down anything that was remotely related to company law were just about nil. So I discarded the question paper and proceeded to stretch my mind in an altogether different direction. I spent the equivalent of two football matches recalling every detail that I could muster of every game from Everton's previous decade of football. Needless to say, I failed the exam (maybe I got some of the crowd attendances wrong!) and it signalled the beginning of a pretty rapid demise for me in that particular career.

More than two decades on, and I still find myself carrying out these memory stretching exercises to keep my mind flexible and to while away extended periods of less interesting times in my life, like bus journeys, exam invigilation or Liverpool matches on a TV where the remote is too remote, if you get my drift.

Last Sunday I had 7 and a half such hours of tedium on an Ethiopian Airlines flight from Addis Ababa to Gatwick. It's my annual pilgrimage to these shores to try to persuade some young, adventurous souls that a teaching career in Uganda is more attractive than life on the chalk face of an inner city comp in Britain which is, actually, infinitely the case in my opinion.

Not being adept at sleeping upright with my knees compressed against the seat in front of me, I decided to set my brain on night vigil. I began to think about the rather bizarre last two seasons in the lifetime of Everton Football Club.

I hope my numbers don't bewilder you too much and I hope that you follow my thread. I realise that not everyone is a maths graduate or, indeed, of sad character like me.

First of all, let's look at the season 2004–2005. A staggering season that ended in Champions League qualification. Up until Christmas we were heading for automatic entry in second or third place but then the wheels didn't so much come off, as the whole crankshaft collapsed. In the second half of the season we won less than a third of our matches (six) and lost over half (10). More amazing, though, was the difference in performance between the first half and second half of individual matches throughout the season. At half-time we led in just six matches in the entire campaign and yet we ended up winning 18. The comparison is particularly stark when looking at our home record where we led in just two matches at half-time (and they were both late on in the season against Palace and Newcastle) and yet we ended up winning 12. On the other hand, we trailed in three home games at half-time but only lost five at the end of 90 minutes. At half-time in our 19 home games we were 9–7 down in total but eventually finished with figures of 24 scored and 15 conceded. In other words we had a second half performance of 17 scored and just 6 conceded. To demonstrate most emphatically the apparently dramatic effect of the half-time cuppa in the Blues' dressing room, if you took our overall first half performances, we would have taken just 41 points in the entire season, whereas, if you took the second half showing in isolation, we would have gleaned a massive 67 points including 21 wins. That would have still only gained us fourth place but it's six more points than we actually ended up achieving.

Season 2005–2006 has been almost the mirror image. It hasn't finished yet, of course, but we have a relatively easy run-in (famous last words) so perhaps we can assume that our good run since the New Year will continue and these statistics won't be messed up too dramatically. Please don't come looking for me after the Charlton game on Saturday, though, if we've sunk in the Valley again as we often do.

In the first half of this season, we had just 17 points and were in serious relegation trouble. In the 12 matches since then we have already accumulated ten more than that and are still hanging on to the faint hopes of a UEFA Cup place. In fact, to give a measure of how good the second half of the season has been, we have an identical record to that of Chelsea since 31 December and we've scored more goals than they have! Furthermore, if you fused together the second half of this season with the first half of last season, we would have 67 points. Put more impressively, we'd be level with Liverpool with a game in hand and just five points behind Man Utd with six games to play... and an easy run-in (Whoops, there I go again). Most astounding, though, is the contrast between the first and second half of individual matches this season. Again, it forms almost perfect symmetry with what happened in 2004–2005; that is identical but opposite, if you get my meaning. At home we have scored 20 goals; 80% of them in the first half. Yes, we have managed to score a meagre four second half goals all season at Goodison. In fact, our second half goals record at 'the home of football' makes pretty lugubrious reading; four scored and 12 conceded. Compare and contrast with a first half record of 16–7. In away games the disparity is not so pronounced but still adds weight to the theory that, either the fitness regime at Bellefield is only designed for players to survive 45 minutes of physical exertion, or David Moyes' team talks are worse than bollocks! The record is scored four, let in 15 compared with a first half of 7–9. If we were to take our second half record only this season, we would have just 27 points and eight goals and be sitting firmly in the relegation zone. Compare this with a first half showing of 48 points which is just five points from a UEFA Cup place and four points better off than our we actually are at this point in time.

In summary, if you had turned up at half-time at Goodison for every league match last season, you would have missed very little in terms of Everton taking a lead or, indeed, scoring a goal; incidentally, not once did we accumulate more than one goal in an opening 45 minutes. This season, you could quite happily have left at half-time content in the knowledge that little else was going to happen as regards Everton goals or success of any kind. Finally, if you combined the results from August to Christmas 2004 with those of 31 December 2005 to April 2006 we'd be currently living in the rarefied atmosphere of possible automatic Champions League qualification whereas, if you care about Everton at all, you would erase 2005 from the record books completely.

So, what conclusions can be drawn from this numerical labyrinth? David Moyes spoke with the inspiration of Martin Luther King over the half-time oranges last season and has been talking out of his orifice this time round? Possibly. The debacle in Bucharest adds weight to that argument. It can't really be put down to fatigue or a lack of stamina this season given that it's virtually the same players as last season except a few more of them. Is it boredom, complacency, attention deficit? Think of the second half of the last three home games against Fulham, Villa and Sunderland compared with the second halves. It does take some explaining. 7–2 aggregate at half-time and three leading positions, 9–4 at full-time with two wins and a draw. And what about this mystical threshold that we have crossed at the half way stage of each of the last two seasons? From the sublime to the inept last campaign; the opposite this. What really changed? The obvious factor to consider is the January transfer window activity. In both years activity was pretty scarce for Everton but there is perhaps one clue to explain our half term transmogrification. In 2005 we brought in Arteta and our form plummeted; in January 2006, Alan Stubbs returned and our results soared. So a granite defender is more valuable than a midfield artist; Stubbs is better than Arteta! And there I rest my case; that statistics is a misspelling of bullshit and a statistician would describe his bodily state as 'On average, I feel fine' if you put his head in an oven and his arse in a bucket of ice. In other words, please rip up this article and just look forward to our easy run-in (sorry!) Easy if we are winning at half-time, that is!

Sorry for wasting your time."

THE STATS THAT PROVE THAT STUBBS IS BETTER THAN ARTETA!

2004–2005   **2005–2006**

	W	D	L	F	A	Pts	W	D	L	F	A	Pts
FIRST HALF OF SEASON	12	4	3	23	15	40	5	2	12	10	30	17
SECOND HALF OF SEASON	6	3	10	22	31	21	8	3	2	21	13	27
TOTAL	18	7	13	45	46	61	13	5	14	31	43	44
FIRST HALF OF MATCHES	6	23	9	14	21	41	12	12	8	23	16	48
SECOND HALF OF MATCHES	21	5	12	31	25	68	5	12	15	8	27	27
TOTAL	27	28	21	45	46	109	17	24	23	31	43	75

And, I really was wasting your time, as that easy run-un produced just three goals and one last minute win in the final six matches, rendering many of these statistics completely unremarkable.

Chapter 9: A Good World Cup for Everton.

(SEPT 2006).

The 2006 World Cup played in Germany was memorable in the early rounds but seemed to peter out the nearer we came to its climax with the almost inevitable conclusion of a final remembered only for Zidane's rush of blood and red card. Well, that was my view of the world's greatest sporting festival of that particular summer. Then again, as you will see from this article, my view, in line with many Evertonians, I suspect, was somewhat disconnected from the mainstream.

"It's perhaps surprising coming from someone with such an 'international' outlook and such a debilitating devotion to football that I should have such a parochial approach towards the national football team. In fact, I am not really interested at all in what happens to England unless there is some Everton representation on the teamsheet. In the club versus country argument, the club wins hands down every time as far as I am concerned. I have now lived abroad for the best part of two decades, but I keep abreast of the English Premier League via the multitude of communication media now available, notably satellite television which allows me a viewing choice of anything up to eight live matches every weekend. Those matches not transmitted live are shown in their entirety as a delayed broadcast so, basically, I can see every minute of every Everton match from the comfort of my living room here in Uganda. For me a weekend like last week's international break induces severe withdrawal symptoms. Only three weeks

into the new season, as well. Just as we're all strapped in ready for another Everton rollercoaster ride, the electricity cuts on the first peak (2–0 at Spurs) and we are left stranded while the electrician is called. Let's hope the ride doesn't resume with a spectacular descent against Liverpool.

I would really like to know, though; am I totally out of touch? Am I so insular to the point of autism or does every Evertonian feel the same? England V Andorra was no substitute for Everton V Anyone as far as I'm concerned. Even the vague interest of seeing Phil Neville or AJ wearing the Three Lions was not sufficient compensation for not seeing those two plus nine others in the royal blue. I might have lived in East Africa since 1989 and traversed many other countries during that time but, when it comes to football, my world begins and ends with Everton F.C. That is why I felt general pleasure from the Germany World Cup and not a tear was shed when England were vanquished with such predictability by Portugal. At the risk of alienating myself from the rest of my fellow countrymen and perhaps condemning myself to permanent exile from the home of my roots, I will now list six reasons to be cheerful over the recently concluded World Cup, apart from the obvious benefit that it did not interrupt Everton's fixture schedule.

1. NUNO VALENTE. My interest in the World Cup fundamentally revolved around two players. If there were two countries that I would not miss watching at all costs, they were Portugal and Australia. As this fanzine is read almost exclusively by Evertonians, I am sure that I need elaborate no further. At left-back for Portugal, with his nonchalant demeanour and floppy hair, Nuno Valente oozed class. In fact, it was hard to recognise him from the player who looked so clueless when he first arrived at Goodison. Even against the world's most talented strikers, our Nuno seemed unruffled and possessed an uncanny ability to compensate for his tortoise pace with pin-point positioning. As we know, a Watford player almost kicked him into Stanley Park in his first game of this season for Everton, so we haven't yet felt the full benefit of this newly discovered vision of elegance on the left flank of our defence, but the World Cup brought a great sense of optimism for us in that department.

2. AUSTRALIA. As stated above the only other team that represented essential viewing for me was Australia. Initially the reason was obvious and when Everton's wizard from Oz rose from the bench to put Japan to the sword in the opening game, almost all my dreams were realised in seven glorious minutes. Apart from Tim's dynamic and pulsating performances on the world stage, though, Australia actually turned out to be the most entertaining team in the whole competition, in my opinion. They played the way an England team should have played; like an English Premier League side, full of passion and heart. They had a big central striker, two wingers and masses of energy and endeavour, mixed with a little naivety which eventually led to their downfall against Italy in the second round. Tim's displays were symptomatic of all the good aspects of the Australian team and, once again, my heart swelled at the thought of him playing like that in the coming season for Everton. Let's hope the corner flags of the Premier League are ready for a battering!

3. AUSTRALIA V CROATIA. On the same theme, I think that Australia V Croatia was easily the most entertaining game of the whole tournament. A combination of the Australian philosophy, the presence of our Tim and the fact that the result really mattered and was in the balance for so long, made it a truly compulsive 90 minutes. But no, I have omitted the most important reason as to why that particular match was so special. The main contributor to this slice of World Cup theatre was the ridiculous Graham Poll who, criminally, is still allowed to continue masquerading as a top flight referee. Here, on the biggest stage of all, he finally demonstrated what we Evertonians have always known, especially after his comical performance in the 'derby' last Christmas, that he really is the most inadequate Premier League referee there has ever been. However, even we hadn't realised that his mental arithmetic skills were less developed than David Beckham's.

4. DAVID BECKHAM. Which brings me nicely on to our dearly beloved England captain; surely the most overrated player in an era when mediocrity has never been so easy to market as talent. Take away his fee-kicks and, let's face it, with enough practice, any player can become half decent with a dead ball (remember Carsley at Newcastle two years ago?), Beckham is left to look pretty inadequate; no speed, can't dribble, can't tackle, can't put a coherent sentence together. As with Graham Poll, Germany 2006 will go down as the World Cup that exposed Beckham for what he really is; an inflated reputation far out-weighing his average ability. It was obvious to all discerning football observers that Beckham was in the team only because Sven was even more infatuated with him than he is with the string of witless bimbos that have trailed the shiny domed Swede for the past five years or so.

5. SVEN GORAN ERIKSSON. Did someone mention our cunning leader? Like Poll and Beckham, Eriksson's monumental shortcom-ings were mercilessly laid bare on the battlefields of Germany. The dif-ference was that, unlike the aforementioned who possibly still had a semblance of professional pride remaining to be extinguished before the tournament began, Eriksson's mercenary lack of interest in the job he was being paid about £12,000 a day to do (and is now being paid £12,000 a day not to do) meant he could smile smugly after the Portugal penalty farce. The same smug smile that he inwardly enjoyed before a ball had been kicked in anger, when he was convincing the gullible English football public of his wisdom to include a Coca Cola league wonderkid* as one of our country's only two fit strikers in the squad; the other being a seven foot beanpole** who is not fit for any squad!

6 WAYNE ROONEY. Talking of unfit England strikers, there was, of course, the former darling of The Gwladys Street, Wayne Money. The tabloid obsession with his broken metatarsal reached such sickening levels that, on one occasion, the question of whether it would mend in time for the fat git to play in the World Cup, became the number one Sky news headline on a day when two British soldiers were killed on active service in Afghanistan; perspective gone pear-shaped, I would suggest. I have a confession to make. When the news guys filmed him getting out of his car to go for that scan in Manchester, I was actually hoping that the car would run over his foot, thus making any X-rays pretty academic; a crushed foot, after all, looks, to all intents and purposes, the same from the outside as it does from the inside. There, I've said it now and I'll probably be turned away at Heathrow, should I ever dare to set foot in my own country again; but, treacherous as it may seem, that was my view on Mr Rooney's foot. Needless to say, when he tried to curtail any thoughts that Carvalho may of had of extending his family and was consequently shown a red card, I was cheering to the rafters. Do I need clinical help or were other Evertonians sharing my joy at that moment as we experienced an unbridled release of frustration borne out of two years of suffering the 'Rooney rise' since he deserted the cradle of Goodison?

So there you have it. I wish I could be more patriotic about football. I am patriotic about many other things; the cricket team, the rugby team, the athletics team, Fawlty Towers, two World Wars, The Sex Pistols, in fact a myriad of different facets of Old Blighty but, when it comes to football, the parochial and tribal instincts kick in. How can I suddenly support the likes of Gerrard, Rooney and Terry, when every weekend I despise their very existence? Can pulling on the Three Lions really cause such a metamorphosis? Not for me, it can't. For me, my club loyalty means I can support Australia ahead of England, I can even support Portugal *against* England and I can reap perverse pleasure from seeing the anguish and torment felt by the masses of drunken, misguided losers who pin their hopes on such worthless human beings as Eriksson, Beckham and Rooney.

So, please, Mr McClaren, start putting Osman, AJ and Lescott in the England team and give me a chance to rediscover my identity, embrace my own nation's football team with open arms again and maybe, who knows, even allow me to face the international breaks with at least an iota of something approaching anticipation.

One final thought to prove that it really was Everton's World Cup. Which is the only Premier League club outside London that can boast of having a former player as a World Cup Final scorer in the past 40 years?"

*=Theo Walcott

**= Peter Crouch

The answer, unsurprisingly, is Everton, as our former central defender, Marco Materazzi, scored Italy's equaliser against France. Steve McClaren, of course, failed to raise the spirits of me or any other Englishman over the next disastrous 18 months but, at least, my derision of the national team was more in key with the rest of my compatriots for a brief spell.

Chapter 10: Everton could rule the world.

(NOV 2006).

We Evertonians, inspired by the knowledge of our rich heritage and confident in our history, believe that there is something definitive about our club that cannot be matched by any other. As the evidence on the field of play increasingly renders this innate feeling of superiority unfounded, we look to other ways to prove that our club is just a notch or two above the rest. Playing the game in a spirit of a bygone age when referees were respected and fair play was as important as the result, was just one way that Everton could perhaps set themselves apart from the grubby majority.

"Globalisation, as we well know, has its down side. For all the opportunities it gives people like me to live a double life, immersed in the sunshine and culture of East Africa whilst, at the same time, having access to every detail of what is going on in my home country, it also brings with it an erosion of national identities, all-consuming multinational conglomerates to tear the heart out of local communities and the facility for evil-intentioned megalomaniacs to peddle their poisonous dogma to vast swathes of the world's population with minimum resistance. Hence, we have the current 'Islam problem' and we also have Man Utd, Chelsea and Liverpool Football Clubs. OK, perhaps it's a little unkind to bracket Beneathus in the same company as Bin Laden, Ferguson and Mourinho, but he is grossly misguided and possesses a dangerous amount of influence over young minds around the world.

By seizing the country's sympathy vote after the Munich air crash and being the first English club to win the European Cup, Man Utd had already won the hearts of much of the British public by the 1970s even when their club nosedived out of the top flight of English football. Even I had a soft spot for them as a child. Perhaps it was because they were so insipid and nondescript and, therefore, no threat on the field, that people could have such a benign affection for the club that once boasted the Busby Babes. It is only since their success of the past fifteen years that this mild endearment has transformed so grotesquely into a deep seated hatred of anything associated with the Red Devils. For me, though, it is globalisation that has turned me so vehemently against them. Building on that expatriate fan base of thirty years ago, they have spread their name and logo into every nook and cranny of this planet like a malignant cancer. Unsuspecting locals in the most remote areas of the world have found their markets and shops infested with replica shirts, towels, key-rings, you name it, with the words Manchester United Football Club emblazoned across them. I was in a craft shop in Mombasa a few years back and, amongst all the authentic ebony elephants and soap stone chess sets, I found a leather wallet with a pattern sewn on the outside in coloured beads. Only it wasn't a pattern; it was those repugnant words of that repulsive football club embroidered across it.

Even though their star has been on the wane for nearly two decades, there is still much Liverpool merchandise to be found throughout the world although, thankfully, no bead encrusted wallets that I'm aware of. Unlike Man Utd, their brand was built up throughout the 60s, 70s and 80s due to achievements on the field and, as long as they do not return to such success, (and, let's face it with Crouch and Sissoko in the team, they are never going to) then their reputation will continue to dissolve into the mists of time. As far as Chelsea is concerned, people across the continents are becoming vaguely attached to this shower of mercenaries through a curious fascination with the antics of their unhinged manager and the fact that every household football name in the world will probably end up at the King's Road if they don't go to Real Madrid or Barcelona first.

Arsenal, of course, have much support around the world but, unlike the other three, their popularity is founded on the venerable criteria of entertaining people with refreshing, exciting and attacking football (contrast with Chelsea and Liverpool), showing no traits of arrogance or pretentiousness (contrast with Chelsea and Man Utd) and they don't work on the philosophy that football trophies can be 'bought' as in the case of all the other three clubs, especially, of course, the new Roman Empire. The other aspect to Arsenal that separates them from the obnoxious trio, is that they have a certain respect for the rules of the game and an appreciation of the concept of fair play. And this is where our own Everton Football Club finally enter the picture. Moulded by an honest, principled manager in David Moyes, when it comes to fair play, Everton are even well ahead of Arsenal. Come to think of it, Arsene Wenger's selective vision over a number of incidents including Eboue's dive in the Champions League Final, does rather undermine their credentials as paragons of virtue, but they still do not generally indulge in the whingeing, diving and fouling practised to such lengths by the inhabitants of the The Bridge, Anfield and Old Trafford.

It was on the opening day of this season that a somewhat left field theory entered my head. It sounds pretty ridiculous but it may just be a way that Everton could exploit the phenomenon of globalisation, tap into a massive fan potential around the world and, assuming the proceeds from the sale of club merchandise do eventually filter their way back to the club that generates it no matter how far flung the place is where the sale is made, make Everton a much richer club into the bargain. What could this idea possibly be to achieve such miraculous results? Here goes.

When Tim Cahill tried to cross the ball in the 82nd minute against Watford at Goodison Park in the first game of the season and hit Chris Powell plumb on the conk, only for the referee to astound everyone with a dramatic pointing to the spot, what would have happened if Everton had refused to accept the decision and insisted on taking a corner instead? Or, to save the complete ignominy of the referee, what if we had accepted his judgment, but then Arteta had stepped up and 'passed' the penalty kick to the goalkeeper or aimed it at the corner flag? We all know that a penalty is awarded if the ball hits the hand of a defending player in his own penalty area. We all know that that patently did not happen in this case, so why shouldn't we take the law into our own hands and compensate for the referee's failing eyesight and ensure justice prevails? Here's another example which I'm sure fellow Evertonians will find much harder to accept: In the 'derby' when Hibbert momentarily played as a second goalie and threw Kuyt's cross behind for a corner, what if our players had appealed for a penalty as vociferously as the Liverpool players did? With 22 players screaming at him, maybe even Poll, stubborn and stupid as he is, would have been persuaded to give the spot kick. I'm not suggesting we become a soft touch and let teams walk all over us; we should still go in hard and receive yellow and red cards for fouls and appeal for decisions if we honestly believe that they should be in our favour, but we do not push referees around and, when we are the beneficiaries of a blatant miscarriage of justice, our players should be conditioned to take the right course of action to correct the error. There have been individual examples of this in the recent past notably Robbie 'Smackhead' Fowler appealing against his own dive at Arsenal in 1997 and Di Canio catching the ball in the last minute when set to score the winner at Goodison in 2000 because our goalkeeper was lying prone on the ground injured. Those are examples of individual players pricked by their conscience in the moment but, what if a whole team were instructed to play by such tenets of good sportsmanship? Such incidents would make worldwide headlines for all the right reasons and Everton could be thrust into the global limelight; a name synonymous with everything wholesome and honourable in the world of sport. Sponsorship deals would flood in from companies and organisations keen to pin their colours to an image of football not seen since the days of Stanley Matthews and flat caps. I often tell kids at school when faced with a barrage of Man Utd propaganda regurgitated from what the media presents to them that 'if they knew their history' they would know that their team cannot hold a light to our glorious Everton. Unsurprisingly this doesn't cut much ice with them and so I go on to denigrate Rooney, Ferdinand, Ronaldo etc for their reprehensible antics. That also doesn't wash with the youth of today but, if Everton really did become as famous as Man Utd, but for being precisely the antithesis of what Sir Alex and his club represents, I really would have ammunition for a proper debate. A discourse on the pros and cons of arrogance, play-acting and a win-at-all-costs mentality versus an adherence to the original values of the beautiful game as foreseen nearly one and a half centuries ago when soccer came into being.

You may shake your head in bewilderment at such an outlandish proposal but it is not impossible. In the very early days of football, such was the intense sense of fair play that pervaded the sport, if a player gave away a penalty for a foul, the whole of the defending team would stand aside to allow the penalty taker to score into an unguarded net because that was the honourable thing to do. Mind you, that was an era when men blindly ran into a hail of gunfire on the mud heaps of the Somme because that was 'the honourable thing to do'. Times have changed. However, as I reach my mid-forties, I find myself mellowing. I still play football here in Uganda and I regularly encounter refereeing of the most appalling standard. Generally the match official marks out a territory roughly enclosed by the centre circle and conducts all his decision making from within these confines throughout the match. Rarely are linesmen, sorry, assistant referees, employed in matches of the standard in which I play, so marginal offside decisions can be adjudicated from as far as 50 yards away. It's a constant frustration of playing football in sub-Saharan Africa but you get used to it; it's part of the culture. But, whereas ten years ago I would find myself arguing with the referee for decisions made against my team only, now I find I am arguing against decisions made no matter which team is benefitting; I'm simply arguing against any perceived injustice, in some extreme cases, even picking up the ball to award a free-kick to the opposition which the referee, from his position on the horizon, and without binoculars, has failed to spot. It confuses players from both sides but, perhaps with my position of seniority, I can get away with it. The tactics of gamesmanship and, let's be blunt about it, cheating that have infiltrated the game to such an extent that most people now benignly accept it, needs to be reversed. Desperate times require desperate measures and it needs a whole team to make a stand.

There would, of course, be two pleasing by-products to this policy of fair play. Everyone in football knows that, short of being battered with a baseball bat by an opposition centre-half, El Hadji Diouf is never ever going to win another penalty in his life. His reputation goes before him (well coached by Liverpool, incidentally) and now referees seem completely oblivious every time he hits the deck no matter how he arrived there. That could now work the other way round; with a reputation for total honesty, perhaps we would have been given at least one of the two penalties at Blackburn or one of the two penalties at Boro' recently. Secondly, the quality of refereeing seems to be getting worse by the weekend and, by taking some of these clear cut decisions out of the hands of our bumbling officials and overruling the man with the whistle and the ludicrous earpiece, we are making them look even more inadequate than they already are. Indeed, it may just persuade Graham Poll to give up trying to referee altogether!"

Could professional football really revert to a sepia tinted age of chivalry and honour?... Let's move on.

Chapter 11: If you know your history.

(JAN 2007).

Perhaps supporting Everton inevitably causes an inclination to the retrospect. Our lack of prospects on the road ahead urging us to constantly glance in the chronological rear view mirror. And what a view it provides. As our signature tune goes: 'If you know your history, it's enough to make your heart go-o-o-o-o-o-o'...

"So, as we reach the middle of January, Everton are in mid-table. True, we are not that far off a Champions League spot but, then again, with Tim Cahill injured, that gap begins to look like a chasm. Once again, we Evertonians are looking at an outside chance of UEFA Cup qualification to keep our season flickering. It's a familiar situation in which we find ourselves in the embryo of another new year but, with the current financially determined football hierarchy that exists in England, one that a majority of Premier League football club fans are resigned to. Most of us are left to indulge in the rather negative pastime of 'inverted supporting' which involves praying for a miracle every time Liverpool, Chelsea or Man Utd take to the field, hoping that they lose and thus giving us all some joy and a sliver of optimism that the football world order is about to lose its equilibrium. Despite all the gloom of another painfully predictable season, though, I cannot lose my passion for the game and I cannot lose my passion for Everton and, with the on-the-field efforts now fizzling out into obscurity for another year, I find myself drifting off into an ethereal blue world attempting to identify the essence of Everton and what makes our club so special. We are one of the 12 founder members of the league, that's true (but

so are eleven others, obviously!) and, since that first season 119 years ago, we've spent all but four seasons in the top flight; a record that no other club can come remotely within touching distance of. It's something to be proud of but, there must be more to explain my attraction to Everton Football Club. The BBC has a rich heritage but I don't have an undying affection for it ahead of all its rivals. Sky might be the broadcasting equivalent of Chelsea; no history, no tradition and lots of superficial, insincere glitz, but I can still support and enjoy watching Sky. So history and heritage alone are not enough to secure my loyalty.

Looking more closely at our history though, one is drawn to a pattern that suggests that somehow Everton are the 'Chosen Club', the one that God shines his light on and has selected as a sign for the world to follow; a portent of something greater than we mere mortals can understand.

When Everton finally won their first title of the 20th century (their second overall), World War 1 broke out. In the middle of our next successful campaign, Stalin was busy assuming absolute control of Russia by despatching Trotsky and 29 other opponents into internal exile. Just five years later we were champions again, just as Hitler gained German nationality paving the way for his elevation to the post of German Chancellor. In 1939, when we won the league again, we were to keep the trophy for seven years as World War Two broke out. In fact, here's a question to put to those 'knowledgeable' Koppites: Which club has been in possession of the league championship trophy longer than any other club? Answer: Everton; 20 years – 13 of them during the two World Wars. Perhaps our influence on the direction of world events was waning by the time of our next league title success in 1963 as it merely came amidst the backdrop of the Cuban Missile Crisis when a third World War was narrowly averted. The uncanny correlation between our club's success and global instability was really diluting by 1970 when our glorious 'School of Science' team took the championship in style, but the only discernible seismic activity on our planet at the time was the disbanding of the Beatles. 15 years later Howard Kendall took our Blues to a record breaking title success, inadvertently, it seems, triggering a reaction in Belgium from some frustrated Reds and, lo and behold, English clubs were banned indefinitely from European competition; FIFA's equivalent of a World War against England, you could say. As we know, that particular event shaped the recent history of football in this country. Everton, 'The Bank of England Club' of the seventies were at the pinnacle of English football which, in turn, had been at the pinnacle of European football for a decade, and now we were suddenly denied the chance to challenge ourselves against the world's elite and make a few bob into the bargain. Where would Everton be now if it wasn't for Heysel? 1987, the year of our last triumph, was also the year of the biggest stock exchange crash since Wall Street in 1929 and signalled the beginning of a world recession.

If the 'Everton effect on world events syndrome' were to have continued, perhaps we should have won the Premier League in 2000–2001 as the catalyst for 9/11, the most recent piece of world shattering activity. As it is, the thugs of Heysel put paid to that; the European ban, not only scuppering Everton's hopes of football world domination, but, it seems, the collapsing wall in Belgium symbolised the dismantling of our influence on global politics, global economics and global peace.

As a superstitious football fan, I can still make my hypothesis fit, though, by adding the caveat that it is a phenomenon attributable within the parameters of the 20th century only. However, there are signs that the power is returning in mysterious ways. Read on:

This quick journey through the last 100 years of the world and Everton Football Club resonates with the day to day life of an Evertonian. You see, we are different. The light of a deity shines down on us. We are chosen people, selected above others. People who have followed the right path. Isn't David Moyes the only manager these days who does not moan about referees and fixture congestion? And strange things are starting to happen to our beloved club again; bizarre goings on unique to Everton. Correct me if I'm wrong, but aren't we the only team in the history of the Premier League to have conceded a goal against the bottom team because our central defender was doing up his boot laces instead of getting in the way of a shot (Yobo at Charlton)? And, in an era when referees are terrified of booking players for diving because Sir Alex, Mourinho or, even Mr Jewell, will give them a slating, we will surely be the only team this year to have a player yellow carded for being blatantly tripped (Van der Meyde at Portsmouth). In that same match at Fratton Park we conceded possibly the greatest volleyed goal the Premier League has ever witnessed. Most eerily, though, was an event that occurred at Goodison Park on Remembrance Day, 2006. With Everton eying third place in our second best start to a Premier League season and a midfielder on the shortlist for European Footballer of the Year, that jinx struck again. No World War this time, no stock exchange meltdown, no emergence of a manic dictator; just the clumsy, clodhopping tackle of Lee Carsley on, yes, our potential European Footballer of the Year, Tim Cahill. If the assault had been inflicted on an opponent, Carsley would surely have been sent off but, instead, as Cahill was being carted off on a stretcher with a rearranged knee, Carsely continued on in his uncoordinated way leaving Evertonians to reflect, once again, on how our highest hopes had been deflated, our ambitions adjusted downwards by the most unexpected happening at the most inopportune moment. There is some hidden power within our club, an endearing propensity to shoot ourselves in the foot or to precipitate an external chain of events, be it the invasion of Czechoslovakia in 1939 or the carnage of the 1985 European Cup Final, to prevent us from capitalising on our footballing success. Even when we finished fourth, two seasons ago, our cheers were instantly shoved back down our throats by our 0–7 debacle at Arsenal and Liverpool producing the flukiest six minutes in their history (or, however long it took for them to score three goals in Istanbul). For a while it looked like our Champions League place would be snatched from us. Did you ever consider that that bolt of lightning that struck on that May evening in Turkey in 2005 was instigated by Everton's supernatural power to inflict agony and frustration on its own supporters and the world in general? It was certainly nothing to do with Liverpool's own ability to play football.

All this history has given Evertonians an unquenchable facility to laugh at ourselves. We are generally intelligent, not noted for mindless hooliganism or moronic chanting. We have humour and an inexhaustible capacity for ironic reflection, philosophically modest even when we know, deep down, that we are actually superior to all other football fans.

Even our players seem to have an instinctive understanding that representing the blue of Everton is an honour not a job and that there is a certain code of conduct to be followed when accepting that honour. Rooney was too thick to understand it but, over the years, Everton players have generally not indulged in the less palatable aspects of the football culture of their day. In the present day, it shows in our respect for the rules and officials, not being girls' blouses and wearing gloves in cold weather and having 'real' goal celebrations full of testosterone or humour like AJ's 3–0 salute in the 'derby'. I recently produced my coup de grace to my 9-year-old son who is a True Blue but, understandably for one so young, occasionally questions his faith. I said to him "Chris, when a goal is scored, Tim Cahill punches the corner flag. When Alonso scores, what does he do?" Chris's expression slowly changed from earnest concern to the bright smile of enlightenment as he answered: "Sucks his thumb, dad". Case closed. Doubts dispelled.

So, while we wallow in mid-table for another season, we can consider the question that, if were to be bought out by an Abramovich type character and we were to buy the league title like Chelsea, are any of us really prepared for the apocalypse now? Because forget your global warming or Al Qaeda, the biggest threat to the future of this planet is Everton winning the Premiership."

And even Alex Ferguson couldn't overhaul our record of 20 years in possession of the league title. How ironic if Mr Moyes should be the one to finally nose Man Utd ahead of us.

Chapter 12: Five year Plan.

(APRIL 2007).

A 2–1 home defeat to Spurs on 21 February 2007, brought the first noises of serious dissent towards David Moyes from the Everton faithful. Believing in the adage, rarely observed in modern football, that continuity and stability might just be the key to success, this article encouraged Evertonians to stick with their manager as he reached his first significant anniversary and be careful what you wish for.

"What were you doing five years ago? I know very well what I was doing, I was just coming round in the dentist's chair after a rather painful extraction, to be told the news that Walter Smith's long, agonising reign as Everton's manager had finally been brought to an end. Yes, my deep routed molar was removed on the same day that Walter Smith met the same fate and, for evermore, I will associate in my mind Walter Smith's tenure at Everton with toothache. The world hasn't actually changed so much since March 2002. Bush and Blair were in power. Okay, the Iraq war hadn't started but 'the war on terror' had begun since the events at the World Trade Centre six months earlier. The football world has changed a lot in that time, though, and, for David Moyes to have reached five years in charge at Everton, is some achievement. Indeed it makes him the sixth longest serving manager in the Premier League and, amongst the five ahead of him, Neil Warnock and Paul Jewell have spent most of their time in charge of their clubs outside the top division. It just leaves Ferguson, Wenger and Allardyce with greater longevity and it is no coincidence that their clubs are well established top Premier League sides. You may think

that, in the case of Man Utd and Arsenal, it is no great achievement, but take a look at the top flight status of those two clubs just before their current managers took over; it was nowhere near as stable and consistent as it is now. So, there's the first lesson to be learnt for all those impatient Evertonians; apart from that one Rooney ruined season, Moyes has started to establish Everton as a regular top 10 finisher. The graph of Everton's final league position in the five years that Moyes has been in charge is a bit saw-toothed but the underlying trend is definitely upwards. As was shown when Phillip Carter stuck defiantly with Howard Kendall in the bleak winter of 1983–1984, that faith in a manager is usually rewarded. You may say that, by Christmas 1983, Kendall had only been given half the time that Moyes has had so far, but the football world has changed dramatically in the last quarter of a century and, more particularly, in the past decade. In those days teams like Watford, QPR, Ipswich and Southampton were regular top five teams with home attendances that barely reached half those of the then 'Big Five' (which included Everton incidentally). There were rich clubs and less rich clubs but the differential was much less pronounced and the old First Division was a much more egalitarian society. Moyes' task is indubitably more difficult than Kendall's was. I'm not alone, I'm sure, in hankering after those days when the top 4 teams at the end of the season could not be predicted with virtual certainty every August as they are now. So, what Moyes has achieved in five years, I would say is pretty much on a par with what Kendall attained in three. The question is, what next?

If we are resigned to the new order then we might as well look at fifth place as the best we can achieve, in which case our present manager is almost there. Like the man himself, though, I am still believing in the seemingly impossible; that Everton can actually break into the top four. Moyes is fiercely competitive and, a manifestation of such character, is that he never knows when he's beaten. Bill Kenwright and his Board must recognise this and stick with him. He must be given at least another five years to complete his job. If, by then, progress is not discernible, then, and only then, should they look for change.

Don't get me wrong, though, Moyes is not immune from criticism and, if he's the man I think he is, he will be the first to admit that he's made mistakes and that there are areas where he can improve. The rest of this article will endeavour to look at how improvement can possibly be achieved, while appreciating that Moyes actually is the right man to fulfil all our ambitions for Everton Football Club.

Rather than look at the statistics that will generally back up the argument that our flame-haired Scot is the right man for the job, I thought it would be better to look at the managers of the clubs that he is trying to emulate and, thus, prove beyond doubt that we really have no reason to covet any alternative. Presumably, as we are concerned with becoming a top four team, we should look at the managers of the incumbent top four. When we analyse their philosophy on football and their vision for their clubs I think you will see that, with the possible exception of Arsene Wenger, we should be very grateful indeed for the appointment that Mr Kenwright made half a decade ago.

Let's start with the top and work our way down. Alex Ferguson is a cynical, manipulative bully with little regard for the spirit of the game. He is, to sporting ethics, what *Eastenders* is to reasoned diplomacy. His footballing philosophy is to put psychological pressure on the referee from the moment of that unfortunate individual's appointment for the next Man Utd match until the end of the post-match interview and beyond, if necessary. Not only will this significantly influence the outcome of the match in question, but it will serve as a reminder to that particular referee to 'behave' in any future Man Utd games that he may be involved in. In addition, there should always be at least one foul-mouthed thug al a Keane, Rooney, Ferdinand etc on the pitch to keep the pressure on the officials during the 90 minutes and to soften up opponents as necessary. Furthermore, the more gifted players are encouraged to dive at every conceivable opportunity to heap further psychological persuasion on the referee and his assistants. In summary, Ferguson's philosophy is to exploit every avenue for cheating but, because he's been knighted, we'll call it good old honest gamesmanship, shall we? And what of his vision? It appears to be to assemble an even more obnoxious group of individuals to eclipse all the objectionable prior versions that have been shunned by fair-minded sports fans throughout the world. How else do you explain Wayne Money's continued existence in their starting 11? Ferguson is too bloody-minded to include him simply to try and justify the 27 million (eventually) that we stole off him for the fat git's signature. No, it is blindingly obvious that the overweight, overrated, smug potato- head fits the Man Utd image and vision to a tee and match officials will continue to be doused in his phlegm whenever they dare to rule against United for many years to come.

Moving down the table we find Chelsea, overseen by 'The Special One'. Special at what, who knows? Mourinho's philosophy is basically to spend as much money as he possibly can and cry when he can't. This spending should bear no relation to the quality of the player being purchased or the needs of the team, hence the outcome that Chelsea began this season with just two recognised centre-halves. Coaching ability is an unnecessary accessory for a manager when he is so indulged by his boss, that he is allowed to buy the best players in the world and, in many cases, turn them into average players. Hopefully, the theory goes, there will be just enough of the squad remaining undamaged by the manager's excessive ego and bizarre concept of man-management, to still be able to win something. Call me a Philistine, but a pile of bricks is just that, a pile of bricks. It is not a work of art. In the same way 11 men in blue shirts running around mainly in their own half of the field acting and diving is just that; men in blue shirts running around mainly in their own half of the field acting and diving. It is not entertainment and it is certainly not football. Regarding Mourinho's vision for Chelsea, it extends to approximately three games. If he wins them, he stays; if he loses them, he threatens to leave, craving the adulation of the Chelsea fans who, being as shallow as they are, will oblige, not quite realising that they have been seriously conned over the last few years.

In third place we come to a bit of light relief. Liverpool's preoccupation with hiring avuncular, pigeon-Englished dunderheads to lead them to the next level is a cause of great amusement for the followers of 'the small team' in Liverpool. In fact, in his first season, Benitez succeeded in finishing below Merseyside's 'village team', a feat not even achieved by his pudding-faced predecessor. Philosophy? That seems to amount to buying criminals or Spaniards or anyone that looks or sounds Spanish and piss off your best players by playing them out of position or not at all. Vision? Very blurred but, in tandem with the plans of the new commercially orientated ownership, can probably be summed up as, hoping Liverpool will go forth and multiply which is, of course, what we all hope. Needless to say *coming* fourth is a lot more likely than *going* forth, in the case of Benitez and his team.

Now, the one team in the whole of the Premier League that I am envious of is Arsenal, and the reason is almost entirely because of their manager. His philosophy is the antithesis of Mourinho's. He believes football is first and foremost entertainment. He believes in taking young players and nurturing them into skilful, thinking individuals. He does the exact opposite of the Chelsea manager, by taking average players and turning them into world class performers. His interviews are well-considered and perceptive and he is ostensibly a modest person; again the complete reverse of the vacuous Mourinho. Wenger recently said he wouldn't want Chelsea's millions because he's more interested in developing youngsters rather than investing in established stars and, I think, he means it. That's where someone of his immense ability would be appreciated at Everton where paying for players at the very top end of the market is not an option, anyway. But I think Moyes has the potential to do what Wenger is doing. He, however, should take the advice that is offered. For example: When you have a talented youngster such as Anichebe or Vaughan, don't be scared to keep playing them. Ingrain a footballing philosophy into the whole squad of 'pass and move' which Arsenal do and which Everton tradition demands. As Brian Clough used to say; the philosophy at Forest is simple; just pass to the teammate in the best position every time and no individual is more important than the team. Football is simple but emphasising how simple it is, is the hardest part. It needs to be indoctrinated right through from youth level i.e. a common thread on which the whole club hangs. That's what Arsenal have done and that's why, even when they put out their reserves, they still play like the first team and annihilate the likes of Chelsea as they did in the Carling Cup Final in all but the scoreline. Finally, David Moyes has no problem in motivating his team and engendering a good work ethic just like all Arsenal teams have, and he's quite prepared to throw out anyone who unbalances that team spirit (please refer to the afore-mentioned potato head), but, where Moyes is lacking, and can learn from Wenger again, is in being creative as a coach. That doesn't mean making bizarre substitutions as some perverse shock tactic to bring the spotlight on yourself, as Mourinho does when he needs another attention fix. It means having the vision to see a change in strategy, formation or even personnel before or during the match that could change the destiny of a game. I first noticed Wenger's genius nine years ago when Emmanuel Petit arrived and looked out of touch and unable to trap the proverbial bag of cement. By the end of the season he was scoring in a World Cup Final. And I saw Steve Bould or Tony Adams suddenly appearing as a centre-forward in the middle of a match. In fact, Adams scored that famous goal against us to seal their champion-ship in 1998 and almost send us to relegation when he appeared from nowhere to volley past Southall. It's imagination like that that wrong-foots opponents and that helps the more eccentric and gifted players express themselves to their full potential like Henry and Kanu. Kanu is an example of an ex-Arsenal player who is still an outstanding indi-vidual after being coached and then rejected or loaned out by Wenger. In fact, you could name almost a whole team of them; Bentley, Lupoli, Bendtner, Song, Stokes, Anelka and so on. That's real coaching for you, that's genius. Moyes is young, though, and he can learn. And, after all, even Wenger is not infallible; didn't we persuade him to spend eight million on Francis Jeffers once?

So, here's to David Moyes' next five years. Maybe on 12 March 2012, instead of waking up from the dentist's anaesthetic, I'll be waking up from a hangover after we've knocked Barcelona out of the Champions'

League. And, it all starts now with the manager bringing through the youngsters, instilling the Everton 'School of Science' traditions from a young age and using his imagination: He could start by trying Beattie as a central-defender and Richard Wrong as a left-back when we next have our defensive injury crisis because they are clearly playing out of position at present!"

Of course, Moyes lasted another six years and never felt the pain of Kenwright's axe despite not winning a single piece of silverware. Was that loyalty taken too far? For most Evertonians, the preservation of our dignified reputation and regular top eight finishes, gives the answer. Shame the prediction about knocking Barcelona out of the Champions League is so laughable, though!

Chapter 13: The Final Third.

(AUGUST 2007).

The first day of a football season brings out strange chemical imbalances in the brain of your average football fanatic. No supporter believes their club will be relegated, everyone thinks promotion or European qualification is at least an outside possibility. Even the fans of relegation favourites can be heard spouting the statistically challenged mantra that 'if we get off to a good start, we could just surprise a few people'. Evertonians are no different, and the third week of August brings high hopes from those following the blue side of Merseyside of Champions League qualification and, may be a cup thrown in over the next nine months. Given the amount of money we had spent in the summer trans-fer window of 2007 and, that that money had been spent on two somewhat unknown quantities in Phil Jagielka and Steven Pienaar, reasons to be cheerful were both limited and misguided. Not enough to deter this particular fanzine contributor, though.

"Much of the discussion throughout this summer and, no doubt, in the bars around Goodison on the first day of the season, was and will be about Everton's lack of activity in the transfer market. Some will say that it is a repeat of the dismal close season of two years ago when we failed to build on an excellent campaign that saw us qualify for the Champions League. Those same people are probably saying that Moyes and Kenwright should stop whingeing about the inflated prices in the transfer market and connect with the real world. They compare them to frustrated first time house buyers who give up trying to grasp a foothold on the bottom rung of the property ladder on the assumption that house prices must come back down into affordable range again

sometime in the future. In the meantime, they remain homeless and excluded from the world of the truly upwardly mobile. It's a fair analogy but, if you take it one step further, you can see that such a prudent approach is probably right. For those who are still intent on joining the rich elite by whatever means and who manage to somehow struggle onto the bottom rung, probably by borrowing six times their salary, and who make it into their first home, they may just find that, within a year or two, they are facing the desolate triple whammy of negative equity, insurmountable repayments and impatient creditors. In other words, they become the personal equivalent of Leeds United.

If we are being honest here, no matter how much money the likes of West Ham, Spurs, Man City and Newcastle throw into the transfer lottery, are they really going to seriously compete with Man Utd or Chelsea next season? Perhaps a better question is: Are they *all* going to compete with them? There appears to be a glass ceiling dividing fourth and fifth place in the Premier League. If all these new members of the rich list with wealthy backers translate their money directly into results, they still cannot all make it into a Champions League position. You cannot fit eight teams into the top four. Some will inevitably be disappointed and then what happens? Given that several of these club owners seem to know little about football, they will be faced with a question that they do not know the answer to. In fact, they won't really understand the question. How can I have spent £50 million pounds on new players and yet my business is only sixth in the league table? The tendency at this point is to revert to more familiar business principles. For such power-hungry individuals, this means resorting to personal intervention to protect their investment. The bane of all managers comes into play; micromanagement from people who think their knowledge of successful business can automatically translate into the creation of a successful football club. The great schism between the manager and the owner(s) is exposed, leading to unrest and quite often the parting of the ways with, almost invariably, the manager being the one to pack his bags. We saw it on a small scale with Mandaric and Redknapp at Portsmouth and we've seen how Hearts have virtually been destroyed by an owner trying to run the affairs on the pitch as well as off it. Even at Chelsea, we have heard rumblings of discontent between Mourinho and Abramovich (which we all pray will continue) despite all their success over the past few years. In the end, these non-footballing people are compelled to reveal their true colours, and the bottom line of the profit and loss account holds more sway than the result on the pitch in a local 'derby' for example. The divergence in the true desires of the fans, the manager and the owners is laid bare and the club starts to fracture. In summary, much of this foreign money flooding into our national game comes with major strings attached. These strings will no doubt be tightened as the euphoric honeymoon periods for these ambitious money makers who temporarily blur the lines between their head and their heart end. Abramovich seems to be readjusting his financial strategy going by the scaling down of Chelsea's spending this summer. I am sure that this will become the pattern for other clubs whose monetary clout derives essentially from a single overseas investor.

Hopefully, that has painted an optimistic picture for Evertonians as we approach a new season; an emotional survival kit for those already depressed at the perceived predictability of the coming nine months or so. And, if I haven't quite banished all the cynicism and scepticism engulfing you, then maybe what follows will do the trick for all those True Blues out there.

Without huge sums of money, Everton, I believe, are doing exactly what is required of the teams waiting in the wings for the 'windfall clubs' to implode. We are keeping faith with a young manager who is learning and improving all the time. We are trying to secure our key players such as Arteta, Vaughan and Anichebe, on long term contracts so that, even if the agreements are not worth the paper they are written on which seems to be the case nowadays, at least we will receive some financial consolation when our prized assets decide to leave before their time is up. We are not allowing ourselves to become dragged into paying silly prices for unproven players and we have a chairman who has a genuine interest in football and, in particular, a passion for the club he is running.

Here are some statistics and a little perspective to convince the doubters. First the perspective: When Walter Smith ended his 'disappointing' reign we were perennial relegation strugglers and had just produced one of the worst performances in living memory in going out of the F.A. Cup 3–0 at Middlesbrough. We had the likes of Gascoigne and Ginola propping us up with their early retirement packages at Goodison. Now, look at our squad and our expectations. Relegation is a word consigned to the history books and our thirty-somethings all *earn* their places in the team such as Stubbs and Carsley. And look at the quality of the manager. For all the criticism that may be levelled at him, which other manager could have elevated a team into the Champions League with the sum total of striking options amounting to Marcus Bent, James Beattie and an injury-ravaged Duncan Ferguson?

The statistics reinforce this perspective. From an average league position of 14th under Smith to an average position of ninth under Moyes. If we delete the season when Rooney's inflated opinion of himself sacrificed the team spirit and we slumped to 17th, the average final position of Everton under our present manager is an impressive seventh.

Looking at last season though, real encouragement can be drawn from how we are closing the gap with the top four. We gained nine points out of a possible 24 against that elite group which is much better than we achieved in the previous five seasons. We scored ten goals which is at least three more than in any of the previous five seasons and conceded 12 which is at least two fewer than any of the previous five seasons. In short, until season 2006–2007 the top four generally wiped the floor with us; last season, Arsenal and Liverpool failed to beat us at all and scored just one goal in four matches against us. We actually took a larger combined total of points off Arsenal, Chelsea and Liverpool than Man Utd managed! Statistics can disguise the events on the field of play and, it's true, that we were perhaps a shade fortunate in drawing at Arsenal and Liverpool. Then again, it was only two 'out of the blue' goals and a goalkeeping howler that turned three certain points into zero at home to Chelsea and Man Utd respectively.

Indeed, losing leads against the top teams was an unfortunate feature of last season. This, however, is where we can glean more optimism. At approximately the hour mark in the eight matches against the top four last season (give or take a few minutes) our record reads: Winning: 4. Drawing: 3. Losing: 1. Goals for: 7. Goals against: 2. This may all appear a little pedantic but analysis of such figures gives significant clues as to what the future could possibly hold. At approximately two thirds of the way through our matches against the Champions League qualifiers, Everton were taking 15 points off those teams. The fact that we collapsed in the latter stages of those games with a 3–10 aggregate deficit must surely be put down to the substitutions that were made. This, in turn, either points to poor decision making by Moyes or, more likely, a superior strength in depth for the opposition. It follows, therefore, that, as Moyes' tactical nous develops which it no doubt will with experience, and our squad slowly but surely becomes bigger, we will indeed, be able to make up that final third.

Football commentators and coaches refer to the importance of the 'final third'. They are, of course, talking about the ability of a team to move from midfield possession to the creation of a goal-scoring opportunity. With Arteta, Cahill, Anichebe, Vaughan and Johnson in our line-up we are making significant strides in that respect. If we could have offloaded Beattie and kept Fernandes, it would have been even stronger. For Everton, though, the most pertinent final third is the last half an hour of every match. If we can solve that conundrum, especially against teams with stronger squads, we may just be able to shatter that glass ceiling and send some of those foreign billionaires back to where they came from."

In the final analysis of Moyes' reign, when he left for Man Utd in 2013, there was another theory put forward as to why we kept failing in the final third of matches; just as we kept failing to grasp countless opportunities to seize our first trophy under his leadership. The word was 'bottle'. Rather like Andy Murray before he teamed up with Ivan Lendl, there seemed to be a fragility in temperament at the time when steel was most needed. Will Man Utd give him that killer instinct or is it something that the manager has to give the team? It was certainly the missing ingredient in the ensuing season when we managed just one point and four goals against the 'Big Four'.

Chapter 14: Yak-a-ty Yak, the Blues are back.

(SEPTEMBER 2007).

The previous article had included a lamentation of our failure to relieve ourselves of the services of the hapless James Beattie. In fact, Sheffield Utd rescued us with a late £4 million bid offering the bulky striker the opportunity to reinvent himself in the more fitting surroundings of The Championship. Having snapped the Yorkshire club's hand off, Moyes then reinvested the money plus a significant amount more making Aiyegbeni Yakubu our record signing. Once we had negotiated the ludicrous immigration rules of our country, the protracted transfer was completed in time for a goal-scoring debut in a 2–1 win at Bolton in September. The omens looked good and this article anticipated another new dawn much brighter than any before.

"I love irony. Like most English people, I have an innate appreciation of the wry humour in situations that turn out to be the opposite to the way they originally seemed to be heading. It's in our literature, our comedy, part of our culture. And how ironic that such great irony is now being visited upon Everton, the team supported by this particular fan of the ironic.

Cast your minds back to the dark days of the mid-eighties; a time for Evertonians to forget. Supporters of our beloved club will assume some sort of historical blunder has just been committed. The mid-eighties represented Everton's halcyon days. Smack bang in the centre of that decade pinpoints our single most successful season ever. The 1984–1985 season included our record points haul, our solitary Euro-

pean triumph and our missing out on a unique treble simply because we were too knackered to play in the FA Cup Final just three days after lifting the Cup Winners Cup in Rotterdam. What could this half-wit be talking about? The dark days, indeed.

Certainly the events on the field give us great memories of wonderful football exhibited on the grass and mud of Goodison at that time. We can all name the squad of 12 (remember there was just one substitute in those days) without the slightest hesitation; Southall, Stevens, Van der Hauwe, Ratcliffe, Mountfield, Reid, Steven, Heath, Gray, Sharp, Bracewell and Sheedy in a 4–4–2 that was as rigid as Howard Kendall's combover. We filed into the Old Lady every other Saturday to be tossed around on the terraces in a feverish tumult as we coaxed out another sublime performance and three points from the men in the Hafnia shirts who seemed to possess telepathic awareness of the location of each other on the pitch and the opposition net. We all recall the heart-warming joy we felt in the pubs afterwards as we reflected on what we had just witnessed; the industry of Bracewell, the guile of Reidy, the cheek of Inchy, the artistry of Sheedy's left foot, the raw aggression of our own Psycho, the elegance of Sharpy, the mesmerising dribbling of Tricky and the sheer will to win of captain Ratcliffe. And the whole team played with the self-assuredness that comes from knowing that the dishevelled, overweight vagrant behind them was actually the best goalkeeper in the world. It all adds up to a nostalgic 'feel good' feeling of the highest order. The only twinge of sadness comes from the realisation that no Everton team has come close to achieving those dazzling standards in the two decades since.

I now request Evertonians to delve a little deeper into your memories. You may have slammed the door shut on this uncomfortable compartment of your brain but I request that you now creak it ajar and peer through the crack. Psychiatrists say that humans have a self-protective instinct to blank out sections of the past that cause us pain or regret. Good therapy often involves confronting our demons and admitting our mistakes to allow us to move forward.

So, please, lie back on the couch and try to remember the following, painful as it may be. "There ain't no black on the Union Jack" being sung with gusto on the Gwladys Street; throwing bananas at John Barnes when he went to take a corner in front of the Everton fans on the Kop; the monkey chants aimed at all visiting black players to Goodison and the fact that we were guilty of all these things because the club seemed to have this unwritten transfer policy that precluded us from signing a black player. Football reflects the society of the time. This is a mantra often trotted out by analysts of sociological trends and moods and there is no doubting that times were very different then. Political correctness was in its infancy and racist jokes were commonplace, even socially acceptable to some people at that time. It was only a decade since 'Love thy Neighbour' had been a beacon of ITV comedy and Alf Garnett had proselytised from his armchair on the ills of open door immigration to a backdrop of ecstatic canned laughter. Even the wonderful Basil Fawlty could not hide his overt shock at having a black doctor attend to him when the moose's head fell from the wall and concussed him. Everton fans in the 1980s had no excuse, though. It was 1978 when Viv Anderson became the first black England international. We should have got over the novelty. The jungle noises emanating from the home terraces of Goodison Park should have long since faded away. But, while all the other clubs introduced black players into their squads, Everton seemed defiant in their refusal to follow suit and so fans identified with this white exclusivity, treating it as some perverse form of collective identity, turning it into a despicable badge of honour. I don't believe I joined in with the moronic songs but I might have smiled at some of the comments and chants and I certainly acquiesced.

I'm lucky, you see. I can open my heart and cleanse my soul in these cathartic juices because I know I am now totally absolved. My redemption is complete because I have lived in East Africa for the best part of twenty years now and I'm married to a Ugandan. Yes, me, the same person who supported that racist club of the eighties has been married for more than a decade to a black lady. In fact, the way some of the expats behave when they come to work in Uganda, it is the whites who I often deride and despise now. The irony is not lost on me. The irony bestowed upon the football club that I have idolised since I was in short trousers is much greater, though.

Firstly there is the ironic twist that, before Everton developed this unsavoury racist reputation of the eighties, we were actually one of the first top flight English clubs to have a black player in our ranks. Does anyone remember Cliff Marshall who played in the first half of the 1975–1976 season? The greatest irony, though, has not yet happened but, I believe, is about to.

We've long since moved on from that shameful era. When Daniel Amokachi was introduced to the Goodison faithful on an August evening in 1994, the eruption of euphoric applause was as much a release of years of pent up embarrassment as it was excited anticipation of what our newly acquired Nigerian World Cup star might produce in a blue shirt. Our record since then regarding black players has been patchy to say the least. For every Campbell, Yobo and Anichebe, there has been a Bakayoko, Nyarko or an Earl Barrett. But on 29 August 2007, Everton paid a club record fee of £11.25 million for Aiyegbeni Yakubu. At first I was shocked by the extravagance shown by the normally frugal Mr Moyes. Then I discovered that the Nigerian striker is just 24 years old and that only Thierry Henry stands ahead of him in the Premier League goal charts for the past four years and then I thought of Shevchenko at £30 million and Tevez at £30 million (or whatever) and Rooney at £27 million and Darren Bent at £17 million and, oh yes, what did Arsenal once pay for Francis Jeff(ears)? And then I saw his strength and his skill and his goal within ten minutes of his debut and I knew that Yakubu is going to be an Everton legend and that he may just inspire Anichebe to be the same.

After twenty years in the wilderness, Everton are finally emerging into the bright sunshine of cup runs and Champions League football and who is the Messiah to lead us to that Promised Land? And what is his colour? What was so good about the eighties, anyway?

YAK: You are King."

If it hadn't been for an horrific Achilles injury a year later, Yakubu might just have become that Everton legend predicted with such confidence in this article. As it was, he was the first Everton player since Peter Beardsley in 1992 to notch more than twenty goals in a season but, otherwise, it was his constant smile and inability to return from internationals on time than gave him legendary status at Everton more than his playing record.

Chapter 15: The rules but not as we know them.

(OCTOBER 2007).

Everton's wafer thin squad already appeared inadequate for us to achieve real success in the league in season 2007–2008 with the UEFA Cup to compete for as well. So, even with the season at such infancy, I found my mind wandering to other aspects of the modern game that were causing me consternation, such as whatever happened to the obstruction rule?

"It's Independence Day here in Uganda and, therefore, a national holiday to celebrate 45 years since "The Pearl of Africa" became self-governing after 62 years of British rule. In yesterday's school assembly in front of 730 pupils I set the scene of ninth October, 1962 by playing the number one song of that week ("Telstar" by the Tornados if anyone is interested) and showing the First Division league table at that time with Everton at the top. Man Utd, Liverpool and Arsenal were trailing well behind and Chelsea weren't even in the division. To such lengths I will go, to try and educate the masses in sub-Saharan Africa on the righteous football path to tread! So, here at my desk, gazing out on to the beautiful Kampala skyline, I have a day off to reflect. As the Headmaster of the largest international school in Uganda, I could be reflecting on what our new teaching and learning policy should be, the schools' development plan or staff recruitment strategy. I could, and perhaps should, be thinking of all these things but, actually, I'm thinking about the last five eventful minutes at St James' Park two days ago. There's much talk these days about the optimal work/life balance. I think I have mine pretty well sorted out. Despite considerable responsibility in my work, I can switch my mind off from the rigours of my leadership role when I'm away from the school premises. I expect that many of us wish that we had David Moyes' job. I wonder, though, whether your greatest social outlet also happening to be your daily work, would not be a little suffocatng and probably unhealthy. Anyway, I'm glad that David Moyes is doing the job he does and I believe he is doing it pretty well.

Those last five minutes at Newcastle were the difference between us going into the international break in fifth or tenth position. If we'd scored a winner which we had threatened to do we would have been on sixteen points. As it turned out, a woeful defensive collapse saw us go down 3–2. I think it was a pivotal moment in our season, even at this early stage. It showed that we don't quite possess the squad to cope with UEFA Cup and league success simultaneously. The poor defending at the end of the match was, as much to do with tired minds as tired legs. There is much criticism from the shower across the park about their supremo's rotational policy, but there's no doubt that fresh legs and heads, at least from the substitutes' bench, can make a difference. In their case, of course, the policy has the sole effect of destroying the morale of players and fans because they all know that their supremo is actually a clueless, bumbling Spanish halfwit. Then again, you probably wouldn't see them lose two goals in the final five minutes of a match following a European excursion.

In summary, I believe that this is a season of choices for the Blues. Not deliberate choices but realistic choices. We either have cup success (and that includes all the cups) and league mediocrity or we go all out for a top five league position accepting that early cup exits are inevitable (although we are committed to the UEFA Cup until Christmas at least). Whichever way it turns out, though, it should be regarded as success and more progress towards getting Everton to where they belong and where they were on 9 October, 1962.

So, with Everton's season summed up in mid-October, what else is there to think or talk about on this pleasant Ugandan afternoon? The school's disciplinary system? Nah, how about discussing the rules of association football?

A few aspects of the way the game is played nowadays particularly in the English Premier League, have been concerning me for some time. Let me share them with you:

1. OFFSIDE: Contrary to general opinion on this topic, I actually think the offside rule is quite simple and does not need to be 'looked at again'. The problem is the complete lack of consistency in which it is applied.

Law 11 states that a player in an offside position will only be penalised if, at the moment the ball touches or is played by a member of his team, he is involved in active play by:

a) interfering with play or

b) interfering with an opponent or

c) gaining an advantage by being in that position.

I think that it should be obvious to any referee when an attacking player is doing any of these things. Interfering with play should simply mean that the ball is being passed to him. Interfering with an opponent should mean physically preventing an opponent from moving where he wants to which, in most cases, would be a foul anyway. Gaining an advantage, therefore, doesn't leave much else other than standing in the line of vision of the goalkeeper. I remember in the 1989 Cup Final when Stuart McCall equalised for us in the 90th minute and Liverpool were complaining that Tony Cottee was offside on the goal line. The ball almost went through his legs on route to the back of the net. On the above three definitions he is clearly not in active play. McCall was hardly likely to be passing to him on the goal line and he wasn't in the way of any opponent. Besides, as I recall on that particular day, Cottee didn't interfere with play and wasn't active for the whole afternoon! Brian Clough made many incisive and perceptive observations about football. It was probably one of the few times in his life that he got it wrong when he talked about offside. "If a player isn't interfering with play, why's he on the pitch?" he used to moan if an offside decision wasn't given.

The final word on offside, though, is about giving the benefit of the doubt to the attacker in marginal cases of a player being level or beyond the second last defender. Giving the benefit of the doubt is not a stated law, of course, but is a directive to assistant referees to err on the side of entertainment and more goals. Even though, as a fan, it is hard to accept when, for example, Agbonlahor's goal stood against Everton last month, I agree with the principle, if the assistant is momentarily caught out of position and is unsure. The question, therefore, is why do 90% of the assistant referees not apply this spirit to the law?

2. DISSENT: My opinion on this unfortunate aspect to our game is, I am sure, a universal one so I do not need to preach to the converted. Just as politicians seem to be the only people to lack the courage or will to solve our social problems when most of the population can see common sense solutions staring them in the face, so it is with the football authorities when it comes to ridding the game of this cancer. Just for the record, Law 12 states that a player is cautioned and shown the yellow card if he shows dissent by word or action. Also a player is sent off and shown the red card if he uses offensive, insulting or abusive language. My questions are, therefore:

Why do these rules not apply to Chelsea or Man Utd? Maybe things will change with Chelsea since the architect of their cheating philosophy has thankfully departed English football. Perhaps we should give the avuncular and faintly ridiculous Mr Grant the benefit of the doubt and hope that he attempts to undo the repugnant culture of intimidating officials that his predecessor inculcated at the Bridge.

Why do players such as Lee Bowyer and Spudhead Rooney ever stay on the pitch for the duration of any match given the rules on dissent as stated above?

What happened to the excellent initiative introduced a few years ago of moving a free-kick forward ten yards if the defending team disputed its award too vehemently? It is not in the official laws; I scoured them, but why not? It works in rugby. Do we just have to accept that rugby players are made of more decent stuff than the hooligans that play with the round ball?

3. OBSTRUCTION: Like the moving of free-kicks forward ten yards for dissent, I had actually begun to think that the obstruction rule had surreptitiously been phased out. However, on scrutiny of Law 12 it can be found:

An indirect free-kick is awarded to the opposing team if a player, in the opinion of the referee, impedes the progress of an opponent. Referees nowadays seem to decide there is either a foul requiring the award of a direct free-kick or nothing at all. Obstruction gives this half way option which could actually take a lot of the pressure off of the referee, especially when the offence is committed on an attacking player in the penalty area. So, why don't they use it? There seems to be an unwritten rule in football that a foul has to be more blatant on an attacking player within the penalty area than outside it for the referee to blow his whistle and take action. The psychology of the referee on this matter is easy to understand. The awarding of a penalty is tanta-mount to the awarding of a goal in most cases, whereas a direct free-kick outside the area has many variables to overcome, such as the wall of defenders standing ten yards away, before a goal results. It requires a whole new level of bottle and conviction from the referee to award a spot kick especially if, in the back of his mind, he is haunted by the prospect of Ferguson's post-match hairdryer aimed in his face. If, for example, shirt pulling could be construed as obstruction; after all it clearly amounts to the illegal impeding of an opponent, then we could have so many more indirect free-kicks within the penalty area instead of this burgeoning blight on our game being ignored. As it stands, if a referee is brave enough to give a penalty for shirt pulling, he is lam-basted by commentators who trot out the old chestnut: "If a penalty is given for that, then there would be fifteen penalties every match". Nothing wrong with fifteen close range free-kicks, though, with the dramatic spectacle of ten or more players lined up on the goal line and a goalkeeper wrestling with team-mates and opponents to get prime position. Ultimately, of course, the real objective would be achieved, as teams would realise that the best solution is to stop grabbing hold of handfuls of opponents' shirts in the first place. Some of these other shoulder barges and 'blocking off' offences that referees readily blow for in the middle of the pitch but turn a blind eye to in the penalty area should also be treated as obstruction as I seem to remember they were in my childhood.

Finally on the subject of obstruction, perhaps there could be a clearer distinction made between shielding the ball and obstruction. I know that possession is 9/10th of the law even in football and, if a defender is first to the ball, he is within his rights to protect it by putting his body between the opponent and the ball to allow it to run out of play for a goal-kick. How often do we see, though, the action of shielding turn into something much more adversarial such as shoving and barging? If the defender is making no attempt to play the ball, I believe these proactive movements should be treated as obstruction. There would be many more attacking free-kicks awarded and the indulging in corner-flag time-wasting that eats up the end of so many games and causes such anguish on the pitch as well as in the stands, would be much more difficult to execute without the concession of an indirect free-kick.

4. ADDED TIME. The only reference to be found in the laws of the game relating to the duration of each match is in Law seven which states that each match consists of two halves of 45 minutes each (unless competition rules allow for extra-time) and half-time should be no more than 15 minutes. Allowance is made for time lost through substitutions, assessment of injury to players, removal of injured players from the field of play for treatment, wasting time and 'any other cause'. My contention here concerns the word that is key to so many discussions about football officiating; consistency. It is conceivable that there could be two identical matches officiated by two different referees and one of the matches will have two minutes added to the end of each half while the other has, say, three minutes added to the first half and five to the second. A lot could happen in the extra four minutes of play that the second referee has allowed. 'It only takes a second to score a goal' as Clough used to say. Things have improved, of course, in the fact that, in the modern game, we are at least informed of the minimum amount of time that is to be added. There is that classic snippet of commentary used in the 1997 film, *Feverpitch* when co-commentator, David Pleat says, as Arsenal enter added time at Anfield needing a second goal to clinch the title: "Of course, no one knows exactly how much time the referee will add on". In 1989 we were still in the position where, once we crossed that 90 minutes threshold, we entered the vagaries of the contents of the referee's head. How often now, though, are there gasps of amazement and exasperation from the crowd and furious finger pointing at watches from the coaches when that electronic scoreboard is raised showing the minimum time to be added? To add to the inconsistency and sense of unfairness, the decision on what is shown on that board is significantly influenced by the wishes of the home manager at places like Anfield and The Theatre of Nightmares.

Why can we not, therefore, have some independent timekeeper for football matches as they do in rugby so that the timing of each half is consistent, transparent and fair?

5. STOPPING PLAY FOR INJURIES: Under Law five, a referee stops the match if, in his opinion, a player is seriously injured and ensures that he is removed from the field of play. The referee allows play to continue until the ball is out of play if a player, in his opinion, is only slightly injured.

The key point here is that it is the referee to decide. So, why do players persist in overriding the referee's authority on this point by choosing to voluntarily kick the ball out of play? At the start of last season this rule was re-emphasised and players were told that they had no obligation to kick the ball out of play in the name of sportsmanship.

A year on and we have drifted back to the old ways; play is constantly broken up every time a player falls to the ground and we restart with the ball being thrown or kicked back to the opposition. When the referees do actually take responsibility and stop play we always restart with a namby-pamby uncontested drop ball. Whatever happened to a good old-fashioned contested drop ball? My request on this matter is to the players, not the referees. Please adhere to the letter of the law and don't take it upon yourselves to decide whether a player is injured seriously enough to stop play. Leaving it in the hands of the referee eliminates inconsistency and stops teams and players being condemned for not displaying fair play when they are actually following the rules of the game. It also stops the use of 'tactical injuries' which I am sure the more unscrupulous coaches and managers encourage. And please, let's make every drop ball a competitive one between two players determined to regain possession for their team.

So, there you have it, one day off work and I've managed to rewrite the laws of Association Football and I haven't even mentioned goal line technology. Indeed, if you peruse the full set of laws of the game, you will see that I am merely tweaking here and there and discussing the interpretation and spirit of existing laws, rather than the advocating of a major overhaul. Many people have been watching the Rugby World Cup over the past month or so. I enjoy watching rugby. One reason is that it makes me appreciate the refreshing simplicity, logic and common sense of the rules that govern our beautiful game and, no matter how much the likes of Rooney, Ferguson, Mourinho and Ronaldo try to corrupt them, they are strong enough to withstand such pressure and have stood the test of time.

Having put the world to right on the field of play, let's now hope that the unwritten rules that seem to govern it off the field are also corrected. The rules that dictate that the only route to success is through a foreign coach and a foreign billionaire investor. Perhaps, one day we can return to a football world reminiscent of the one of 1962 that I so fondly recalled in front of all those children and parents and teachers yesterday afternoon on a school field somewhere near the Equator."

In the five years since this article was published, the path of modern football has become even more laden with iniquitous foreign currency, skewing the playing field further. I am proud that Everton remains detached from that world and ploughs its moderately successful furrow with limited funds and a dilapidated stadium. Something at my club will change eventually, though and I look forward to financial meltdown al a Portsmouth or financial windfall al a Man City with equal trepidation.

And, oh, yes; sorry to sound like a cracked record, but where did the obstruction rule disappear to?

Chapter 16: Seventh Heaven.

(DECEMBER 2007).

Autumn 2007 saw Everton in a free scoring, points totting run that reminded Evertonians of the mid-eighties. Having caught our breath from the 7–1 trouncing of Sunderland, we needed to fill our boots with lead and get back to terra firma quickly. Evertonians just don't do 'happy' and this article restored equilibrium with the sobering thought that our joy was destined to be short-lived.

"I told you so. After all this time, are you finally going to believe me? You just laughed and assumed that the African sun had fried my grey matter or that I was simply so far away from the action on the field that I was out of touch. Well, now perhaps you'll have to sit up and listen. I mean, haven't I been the one who has been banging on about how Everton are heading in the right direction? Haven't I been nauseating you with sickening optimism, seeing the football world through blue-tinted glasses? From the moment Potatohead walked out on us in August 2004, haven't I been the one that said it was a blessing? Didn't I say that the team is greater than the sum of its parts? (Or as Roy Keane intriguingly recently observed: "Good players don't make good teams".) Yes, it was me and, now that we sit on a run of ten wins in twelve games and approach the New Year still competing in four different competitions, who was right, eh? Just answer me that, will you?

So, now that I have your attention (you can tell that I'm a teacher), listen to this. I am seriously worried about the rest of the season. No, honestly, I'm not joking; I have major doubts about what is in store for our beloved Blues over the next five months. I'm not talking about our lack of strength in depth or perhaps our lack of quality in certain key positions like at centre-half when Yobo frolics off to this great continent where I currently live for the African Cup of Nations. I'm also not referring to a possible lack of depth in the management department now that Alan Irvine has decided to try his hand at being the top man at Deepdale. No, there are other reasons why I'm apprehensive about our immediate prospects. My problem is that, apart from being a blind optimist when it comes to Everton, I am also afflicted by another odd condition. My problem is that I have an almost photographic memory for Everton results. My recall of other things isn't so hot. You ask me about a conversation in the pub last weekend and details are sketchy (other factors could be in play there, of course), and you ask me where my car keys are a matter of minutes after I've put them down somewhere and I go off in a frantic, curse-laden search for them blaming everyone and everything in sight including myself for my infinitesimally small memory capacity. But you can then ask me about the last time Everton reached the semi-final of the League Cup and I can tell you instantly that it was a 4–1 aggregate defeat to Arsenal in February 1988 and I can even recall Adrian Heath's goal on that soggy, windswept night at Highbury that fleetingly brought us back into contention before Arsenal went on to make it 3–1.

So, when an earth-shattering result comes up like Everton 7 Sunderland 1 as it did on Saturday, 24 November 2007, little cogs in my brain instantly whir into overdrive to retrieve similarly extraordinary scorelines from the archives. Of course, the archives only extend as far as when my brain began storing such data which was when I was baptised into the Good Faith around springtime of 1970.

The results of this search rapidly brought up two other Goodison avalanches in the league. In November 1971 we beat Southampton 8–0 and almost exactly 25 years later we destroyed the same hapless opponents 7–1. What I could also trawl from my memory was that these two dramatic successes, not only arrived 'out of the blue' if you'll pardon the pun, but also signalled the beginning of the end of the season for Everton in both cases. I will now admit that, for the rest of this article,

I am no longer relying on my own powers of recall. I needed more detail to add flesh to the bones of this strange phenomenon, so a reference book or two of Everton's history has been employed. First of all, it is worth comparing the almost eerie similarities between the three freak results. They all occurred in middle to late November; in fact, all within eight days of each other on the calendar. The opposition on all three occasions wore red and white stripes. In the two matches against Southampton, the opponents narrowly missed relegation at the end of the season, so there, perhaps, is a good omen for the Black Cats. On those two occasions Everton finished the season in 15th place and were flirting with relegation with a few matches remaining. And that is where the portents of doom start to haunt me. Just listen to these other dismal statistics. After the 8–0 win on Saturday, 20 November 1971, we went six games without a win. The next two home games saw us draw with Stoke City and Huddersfield Town who both finished below us at the end of the season. We actually only scored eleven more goals at home for the remainder of the season and only won three league games out of 24 altogether in the remaining 5 and a half months. The fall from grace after the 7–1 win against Southampton on 16 November 1996 was equally precipitous. As a result of that annihilation of the south coast team, we went fourth in the league. It was 1 February before we won another home game. We lost six matches in a row around Christmas and won just five out of 26 league games up to the close of the season. In 1971 the season ended with Harry Catterick suffering a heart attack; in 1996 Joe Royle didn't even complete the campaign in charge. Joe didn't suffer ill health but much of his squad did and the consequential poor results forced him to quit. Ironically it was the same Joe Royle who scored four goals in that 8–0 execution of the Saints a quarter of a century previously. There were early exits from the two domestic cup competitions in both seasons but, interestingly, a good result against Liverpool came next to both of the Southampton trouncings. On November 13, 1971 we beat the Enemy 1–0 at Goodison while on the Wednesday following the 7–1 win in 1996 we drew 1–1 at Anfield.

So, a massacre by the Blues in November does not augur well for the immediate future. We, perhaps, don't have quite the capacity for false dawns on the scale of, say, Newcastle Utd or Manchester City but I think Evertonians all know that there is something inherently dangerous in getting carried away with anything when it comes to the results of our team. We've been hurt too many times before to be foolish enough to expose ourselves to the possibility of crushing disappointment. Then again, isn't that exactly what we are doing at the moment? Like young lovers who never learn the lesson of rejection, we believe that we can't possibly be hurt this time, because this season really is the one when our trophy drought ends. I know that's what I'm thinking. Am I wrong to believe that this time we have something of more substance to cling on to than mere wishful thinking? Isn't it true that our resolve is stronger than it was for those two teams from 1971 and 1996, that our capacity for late goals, the strength of our squad, our striking options and even our manager are all better than in those two seasons? Surely these are all facts that should override any statistical superstitions. Anyway, as I write this, we have already gone five matches beyond the 7–1 destruction of Sunderland and not lost any of them. Yes, this really is different, isn't it? Please, someone, reassure me. I am not to be emotionally deconstructed again, am I?

The funny thing is; when I sift through almost 28 years of Everton history in my head for the times that we *conceded* seven goals in a league game, I come up with one 'success'. 7–0 against Arsenal at the end of the 2004–2005 season. The only season in our history that we qualified for the Champions' League! Supporting Everton really is a complex and hazardous business!"

There was no calamitous falling off the cliff on this occasion and season 2007–2008 remained pretty well on track but still the trophy cabinet remained bare.

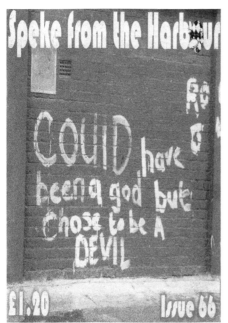

Speke from the Harbour

COUID have been a god but chose to be A DEVIL

£1.20   Issue 66

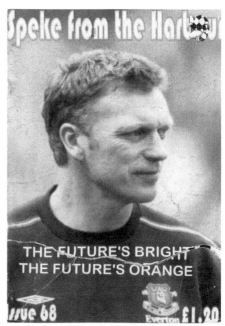

Speke from the Harbour

THE FUTURE'S BRIGHT
THE FUTURE'S ORANGE

Issue 68   £1.20

Speke from the Harbour

Issue 70   £1.50

Speke from the Harbour

£1.50   Issue 72

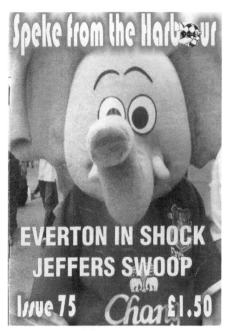

Speke from the Harbour

BRAGGING RIGHTS

Issue 81   £1.50

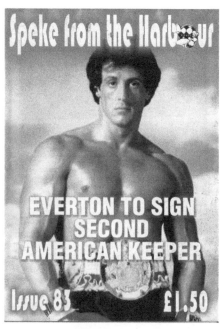

Speke from the Harbour

EVERTON TO SIGN SECOND AMERICAN KEEPER

Issue 83   £1.50

Speke from the Harbour

Issue 85   £1.50

Speke from the Harbour

Issue 87   £1.50

SPEKE FROM THE HARBOUR

YOU'RE FIRED!
Justice for the
Goodison 40,000

Issue 101 £2

Speke from the Harbour

Issue 95 £2

Speke from the Harbour

FIRST SUMMER SIGNING
FINALLY UNVEILED

Issue 97 £2

Speke from the Harbour

SAVED BY THE BEL-GIAN

Issue 99 £2

SPEKE FROM THE HARBOUR

EXCLUSIVE SPEKE PREVIEW!

NEW HOME KIT?

issue 108

£2

SPEKE FROM THE HARBOUR

£2
issue 109

5 MORE YEARS!

Everton

SPEKE FROM THE HARBOUR

HEY MA, I'M ON THE XMAS COVER OF SPEKE!

Chang

issue 111

£2

SPEKE FROM THE HARBOUR

issue 112

FORM IS TEMPORARY...

£2

Chapter 17: The missing ingredient is in the seven Cs.

(FEBRUARY 2008).

Oh, so close! Two single goal defeats against Avram Grant's Chelsea in the Mickey Mouse Cup (the name of this competition always reverts back to its disrespectful title once Everton have been eliminated!) semi-final meant the closest whiff of glory under Moyes had been blown away. While the difference between ourselves and Chelsea was wafer thin, there was a certain inevitability that their superior know-how and quality would just see them edge us out. So, how could we go that extra step to turn those fine margins into dust?

"I tend to hang on to David Moyes' every word these days. Meal times, conversations with the kids, reading of the newspaper, even a visit to the toilet are all temporarily suspended when the ginger one appears on the TV. There is a scramble for the remote control and the TV volume is doubled as my family is forced to listen to his thoughts about the next game, the last game or anything else that he has a view on. If we have visitors, they are not spared this social paralysis, as they find the room falling silent and everyone's gaze turning to the television screen. In truth, much of what he says is pretty predictable. It's rare that he espouses any opinion that any other manager couldn't have fathomed. The media intrusion these days is so continuous that, quite often, the players and managers and coaches have very little original material left to say. We snigger at cliches like 'one game at a time' but, at the end of the day, (whoops, there's another one!) what else is there left to say? Of course, the reason that David Moyes still captures my

attention like no other, is that every word he says is going to have some connection with my beloved football club as he is the face of Everton. Having supported the club for 38 years, I think I can sense when someone has a genuine affinity for the Blues; I can detect whether he has a knowledge of the history and tradition of the club and I can tell whether he has an intuitive understanding as to why Everton is simply the greatest football club anywhere in the world. It transcends results, it has nothing to do with the number of trophies in our cabinet; it is simply an innate feeling that, following Everton is the right path to take. Committed followers of faith, whatever it is, understand what I am referring to. I believe that David Moyes has made that journey and is now as true an Evertonian as you will ever meet, and I really wish we could meet. Whenever I see him on TV, I want to start up a conversation with him. This was particularly true after our defeat to Chelsea in the Carling Cup semi-final. He was patently as distraught and subdued as the rest of us but, as he conceded that we weren't quite good enough, he went into a reflective mood and said that we still hadn't bridged the gap between the top three and ourselves. He then went on to say that we have to find that missing ingredient that will make up the difference. The fact that it is now a top *three* and not a top four is music to all our ears, of course. I didn't understand this morning when Sky Sports News proclaimed that there were only six teams from the Premier League left in the FA Cup; Portsmouth, Middlesbrough and the 'Big Four'. Had they already forgotten that we had lost at home to Oldham in the third round? The same channel had made enough of that depressing result at the time. But, I digress. The point is that, when our orange beacon sent out that SOS for the missing ingredient, I felt an uncontrollable compunction to try and find it. Anything to get our team into an automatic Champions League berth, I was willing to do. If I could just find what is required to make up the six points on Chelsea, I was willing to search day and night; whatever it took, I was going to help our Dave. He hasn't had an assistant for a while; he clearly needs a bit of support and, after nearly a week of searching, I think I have the answer. Davie, my friend, the answer is in the Seven

Cs. Now listen carefully, and concentrate at the back! In fact, concentrating at the back is our first problem.

1. CONCENTRATION. When I watch Everton, I believe every goal conceded is preventable. It's hard for me to bring myself to say "good goal" when someone has the Everton net bulging. Take that semi-final as an example; to me, all three goals conceded over the two legs were down to massive lapses in concentration on our part. Who left Short Wrong-Phillips with the whole of our penalty area to play in on his own for the first goal? (And he still nearly missed it. Great goal, my arse!) Then, why did Joleon, of all people, go to sleep in the final minute to allow Short to outjump him? In the second game, why couldn't Valente be awake enough to see Malouda's hopeful punt from close to the half way line. Even the reactions of a rabbit in car headlights would surely have allowed him to get a block in on Cole's shot. Pienaar's stupid 'tackle' on Giggs at The Theatre of Nightmares before Christmas and Jagielka's similar suicidal act against Arsenal's Eduardo and the litany of Yobo 'moments' are all evidence of why we lose crucial goals at crucial moments against crucial opponents. Our players are generally good enough but, Dave, you've got to make sure that, once you switch our players on at the start, the batteries don't suddenly fade during the game. And one final thing on concentration; can you tell Tim Howard that, when you say you don't like divers, it does not apply to goalkeepers! Matt Taylor from 40 yards, Drogba from 30 yards, even Ronaldo just before Christmas. You know what I'm talking about?

2. CONSISTENCY: If the issue of concentration is addressed, then consistency should follow. When you hear statistics like Arsene Wenger has never lost to a lower league team in his 11½ years at Arsenal and Chelsea haven't lost at home to English opposition for nearly four years, you realise the true definition of consistency. Apart from eliminating the lapses in concentration, though, access to a large squad can help. If a player loses form or is injured, a replacement can seamlessly smooth over the gap that is left. But, Dave, you have to make more use of that. We now have a situation of almost two players for every position on the field; sometimes it requires the following C to make full use of it.

3. COURAGE: Tim Cahill is my favourite Everton player; I idolise him and received the number 17 replica shirt as a Christmas present. However, I think we all have to admit that his form since the goal at Old Trafford has been poor. With Yakubu unavailable for the second leg against Chelsea and Everton needing at least one goal, surely we should have gone with Anichebe or Vaughan alongside Andy Johnson against the best goalkeeper in the world and the tightest defence. Dropping Cahill for one of the young strikers would have required courage but such bold decisions are required sometimes. Also, when it was clear that Valente was having a nightmare coping with Cole who, let's face it, was their only decent player in front of their back five, he should have been hauled off with Stubbs brought into the centre of defence and Lescott switching to left-back. The successful managers make such substitutions with no consideration for shattered egos. We now have the squad so, please, Dave, have the courage to utilise it.

4. CONVICTION: I'm not talking here about the type of thing that Joey Barton receives on a regular basis, but the psychology of actually believing you're good enough. By not having the courage to unleash two out-and-out strikers on Chelsea in the second leg, it sent a message that we weren't really convinced that we could pull back the deficit. From the early stages of that match, I felt that we weren't going to score. That feeling was transmitted from the teamsheet and the way the team was playing. I have tried to like Chelsea since the undertaker replaced the unhinged as manager but I have failed; they still remain arrogant and dull and, I have to concede, deserve the sobriquet, Cheatski. One thing they always manage to do is drag the opposition down to their level. They have an unwavering belief that they will not lose no matter what means they use. At Goodison they had conviction; we didn't. Wasn't there also a certain inevitability about Man Utd and Liverpool scoring last minute winners against us recently in the league? I know that I always get this debilitating sense of dread when we reach the closing stages of tight games against the teams near the top and I think that that feeling comes from years of not winning anything. It's a chicken and egg situation; conviction comes from winning silverware, silverware arrives when we show conviction. I'll leave you with that conundrum, Dave, but it's your job to convince our players that they are good enough to compete with the best.

5 CREATIVE THINKING: The fleeting five minutes when we looked like we might actually score against Chelsea at Goodison, began when Arteta pulled his free-kick back to Neville to shoot. The element of surprise even caught out the smug Chelsea rearguard. They had anticipated another whipped free-kick into the box. They had no idea that Neville was our secret weapon or that he was capable of hitting the target from that distance (in common with many Evertonians, I don't doubt!) That creative thinking can wrong-foot even the most self-assured defence. We had so much possession in the early stages but came nowhere near scoring. Where was the long cross-field pass to change the direction of the attack? Where was a long shot out of the blue? Just something, anything unexpected, unpredictable to surprise the opposition. Malouda did it to Valente. Game over.

6. CAPTAIN: Another Christmas present of mine was *'Sharpy'*, the autobiography of Graeme Sharp. It was wonderful to read of that fabulous team of 1984–1985. I attended virtually every game of that season and that team had all the above mentioned Cs in abundance but, what they also had were leaders. We could see it from the terraces but Sharpy confirms it; Reidy, Gray and Rats were all natural leaders. They brought conviction and consistency. We hear constantly that the Everton dressing room has the best spirit that it has had for a long time. Thank you for creating that, Dave, as it is a well known fact that good morale leads to increased productivity. It can be seen on and off the pitch; the camaraderie, the commitment to long contracts and the general positive vibes coming out of the club all the time. But are there any true leaders? Phil Neville has the character but not the playing ability; Joseph Yobo has the ability but not the character. The priority over the next six months is to find an outstanding captain. It may come from within. Is Joleon Lescott of the right mental fibre? Or, maybe, we have to break the bank again in the summer to go and buy one. I've no idea where from, but we definitely need a John Terry type character to instil a winning mentality into the squad. So, Dave, make it a priority. We need someone of your personality *on* the field as well as off it.

7. CROWD: This one is out of your hands Dave, but perhaps you could get the powers that be to consider the following: I live a long way away here in Uganda, so almost all my viewing of Everton comes via a satellite onto a flat screen that sits in the corner of my living room. Even from such a remote vantage point, I can tell that Goodison Park creates a special atmosphere especially in night games. I was at the Bayern Munich game of 1985 and my flatmate at the time who was working late in the university labs on his PhD that night, said that he could hear the cheering of our goals from where he was. That must be a full four miles away. The Everton fans are special but The Old Lady inspires us. I can't believe that some faceless, soulless Tesco's Stadium will engender such feeling wherever it is built. However, I appreciate the economic arguments for the need for change etc. Surely, though it is not beyond the wit of modern architects to replicate the design of the Goodison Park stadium but, with an extra 20,000 seats and without the obstructed views. We could even build another church in the corner. And it should be called something like The New Goodison, not carry a tacky sponsors' name. Our crowd and stadium are worth a great deal. Decibels can be worth more than dollar bills for a football club. We shouldn't lightly turn our back on such assets.

David Moyes, sir, if you have read my previous articles, you will know that I rarely criticise you. In fact, you stand as a hero to me as the guardian of our great club and I wish you longevity in your current post but, maybe somewhere amongst all my meandering deliberations

here, you can find that missing ingredient that will put us up there with Arsenal, Man Utd and Chelsea.

You completed your post match interview after our Carling Cup elimination by suggesting that the missing ingredient might be another C. You said that maybe CASH was the problem. If that's the case, Davie, pal, then we're knackered!"

And, probably, finance is the most significant missing ingredient. Money talks loudest in football nowadays; in fact, it shouts. But I can't help feeling that Mr Moyes' tenure could still have been decorated with at least one winner's medal with more of the missing ingredient No 4. Clubs of much lesser means than us won trophies from 2002 to 2013 with a display of belief and a winning mentality when it was most needed. We always seemed to suffer stage fright, when 90 minutes from destiny.

Chapter 18: A season of hope.

(APRIL 2008).

One of those lesser teams was Portsmouth who beat Cardiff City in the FA Cup Final of 2008. As we approached this finale of the underdogs, an atmosphere began to pervade that there was life outside of the 'Big Four' after all and that supporters of all other clubs should not yet abandon hope.

> "Here in Africa, the concept of time is different to the one we understand in Western cultures. Nobody here remembers birthdays or anniversaries and the calendar date for an appointment or meeting or a party may be accurate but the time stated on the invitation is very much a ballpark figure; a rough guide to the earliest conceivable time that the event may begin. When you wait an hour for the groom to turn up at the wedding you were invited to, you can be sure that the bride is still mid-perm in the hair salon and you have no one to blame but yourself for being daft enough to actually believe that the time stated on the wedding invitation bore any relation to the actual time that the nuptials would commence. The President of Uganda, like many people on this continent of his generation or older, does not know his exact date of birth but can estimate it by a combination of the season at the time of his birth and the number of good harvests in his lifetime, or bad ones for that matter. Time is an approximate commodity which should not have specific numbers attached to it; it is ethereal and malleable and fuzzy round the edges. When we talk about the seasons in Africa we do not talk in clearly defined terms like spring, summer, autumn or winter, we talk about the dry season or the wet season and, with global warming playing havoc with the earth's equilibrium, these

periods of time are increasingly more random splodges on the calendar. The hundred days of genocide in Rwanda is referred to, in these parts, as the 'season of blood'. If you asked someone here, though, including a Rwandan, when exactly that season occurred, they would be hard pressed to tell you that it was 1994, let alone that it began on 6 April of that year. The exact time and year are simply irrelevant; it was just a period of harrowing trauma and horror that occurred somewhere in the quite recent past.

This short treatise on the meaning of 'African Time' may help some of the less culturally astute Evertonians out there to understand why Yakubu seems a little slow to close down opposition defenders and, indeed, find his way back to Merseyside after three weeks in Ghana, or why Yobo gives the impression that he has all day to make his mind up over that clearance or pass. To these guys, time simply has different parameters to the ones we are used to.

With this outlook on time, comes a lazy memory and, consequently, less appreciation of history. It, therefore, goes some way to explaining why much of this continent supports Man Utd, Arsenal, Chelsea or Liverpool. History means nothing in football as it means nothing with everything else. These teams have been successful in the recent past and, therefore, they are the only teams that matter. The other sixteen teams in the Premier League are an irritant. If many Africans had their way, the league would be contested by just those four teams; the whole season would consist of Grand Slam Sundays and Saturdays and even Grand Slam Mondays, Tuesdays and Wednesdays.

In many ways, though, the same view is held by other poorly informed observers of English football around the planet. That is why the '39th game' was a non-starter. With all the creative marketing in the world, you would not be able to sell Reading V Wigan Athletic to the Chinese, Americans or Australians. In fact, on reflection, it would be pretty hard to sell it anywhere outside the towns of Reading and Wigan.

That last comment was intended to be frivolous. The fact is, the real football fans know that such a match is important because, if the likes of Reading and Wigan didn't exist, there wouldn't be a league. Similarly, the three leagues below the Premier League are crucial as are the non-professional leagues that feed into them.

So, while the uneducated masses exist on a solitary diet of 'The Big Four', the rest of us enjoy the rich fabric of the entire football cosmos that forms the bedrock on top of which that elite quartet smugly perch themselves.

True football fans also have a different way of measuring time compared with everyone else. We also talk in seasons. Our seasons, though, stretch from August to May. I can partition my life off in seasons; whole winters are determined by the progress of Everton. There is a definite glow when I think of the winter of 1984–1985 whereas 1997–1998 appears in my memory in black and white, as some dull, miserable photo of the bottom end of the Premier League table. I should also say that it may bear little relationship as to how the rest of my life was faring at the time; in fact, there has been a curious *inverse* relationship between my personal life and the success of Everton. The mid-nineteen eighties were actually a pretty desperate time for my love life and my career, whereas I was in the full flush of early marital and parental bliss when Everton needed snookers to avoid relegation on the last day of the season in 1998. Quite often an Everton result has lifted me out of despair or plunged me down to earth when life has looked promising. I'm sure Derby County fans will, forever, remember 2007–2008 as a desperate time irrespective of what wonderful successes they may have experienced in their personal lives at that time. As football supporters, the affairs on the pitch colour our lives off it. As Evertonians, the events on the hallowed Goodison turf dictate our mood and our approach to life. If Everton win, we feel we can confront every problem with confidence and a solution; when Everton lose, we feel that the act of even rising from our pit the next day is a pretty pointless one.

That is the world of the true football fan, the one who implicitly understands the meaning and purpose of the beautiful game, the hardy souls who ride the emotional roller coaster of supporting teams that have no guarantee of winning silverware at the end of the season when the starting gun fires in August. Sadly, the sense of exclusivity of 'The Big Four' has allowed the members of that elite group to cushion themselves from this real world of what football was meant to be when it was invented all those years ago. The characters that participate for the 'boresome foursome' are allowed to get away with their selective vision and damning comments where others cannot. Hence, Aliadiere is given a four match suspension for a playful brush with Mascherano, while the Argentinian, with his 'big four' protection can retaliate with impunity. Ashley Cole suffers no ban at all for a calculated attempt to end Alan Hutton's career which he compounds by then treating Mike Riley like a piece of shit. (Come on, now, there's no need for that!). Mascherano was only sent off against Man Utd because Ferguson holds more sway over referees than even the other three in their mini-hierarchy. The supporters of this self-satisfied quad have also developed an arrogant superiority that has no place in an industry that goes under the name of sport. The Neanderthals that follow Chelsea, when they can be bothered to support their team at all, end up eulogising their erstwhile demented cheat of a manager instead of supporting the hapless incumbent and his players. What must those same halfwits have thought when their Ivorian mercenary reversed the scoreline against Arsenal within twenty minutes of them singing that dirge entitled "Josay Moron-eo" in a recent match? Sorry, what a ridiculous concept; a Chelsea fan with the capacity to think.

The whole idea of 'The Big Four' is, therefore, plainly detrimental to the welfare of our wonderful game. It allows millions of fair-weather fans around the globe to believe that the league begins and ends with the Champions League places. And those four snug little slots provide a comfort zone for its occupants that allow them to become even more rich and obnoxious than they already are, insulated from the adversities that the rest of us have to endure.

Suddenly, though, there is something extraordinary infiltrating the status quo. In the last few months there have been strange goings on in the English football world. Goings on that could make this period in our history forever be known as the 'Season of Hope'.

Referring to the football supporters' definition of season, it extends from August 2007 when Man Utd had their worst start to a Premier League season. Soon afterwards, Mourinho was finally, mercifully banished from our shores, hopefully never to return. Using the African definition, though, the 'season' can be narrowed down to the last few months. In that time we've had the Mickey Mouse Cup won by a non-member of 'The Big Four' for the first time in six years, we've had an F.A. Cup semi-final line-up with no trace of the awful four with Chelsea and Liverpool extinguished by a bunch of unlikely Tykes and we've had Man City doing the double over their methane inducing city rivals while Arsenal haven't won a league game for six weeks. We've also had Everton evoking memories of that fantastic 'Bayern Munich night' with their slaughter of Fiorentina in the UEFA Cup second leg.

What would truly make this a 'Season of Hope', though, and the reason that all true football fans around the world should be praying for an Everton win on 30 March against Liverpool, is for our Blue Boys to cross that sacred threshold that separates fourth from fifth and sit above our illegitimate cousins from across Stanley Park on 11 May. Unfortunately, Benithez, in recent weeks, has accidentally discovered that Torres is actually more than just a pretty face (and let's be honest, his face is very pretty). The rotund Spanish waiter has uncovered the fact that, without Torres, even Waterlooville posed a major threat to his team. Consequently, the Spanish goldilocks, having been rested for half a season, is fresh and angry, his feminine pride piqued, and my feelings about our match against the Norwegian supporting American franchise are no longer as upbeat as they were a month ago. But, if we can get the result the whole of civilised mankind craves, and, in the process, reverse the 'Clattenburg Gap'* that has opened up between us, the springtime of 2008 may well go down in history as the season when English football was irreversibly rescued from its apocalyptic predictability."

*Reference to the infamous 'derby' of October 2007 officiated by Mark Clattenburg, won by Liverpool.

Inevitably, Yakubu went to sleep and Torres struck to settle the game at a very hostile Anfield in the first five minutes. Everton looked jaded and only just struggled into the UEFA Cup for the second consecutive season.

Chapter 19: Round in circles.

(AUGUST 2008).

Close season activity at Everton was virtually non-existent. Our only 'signing' by the first day of the 2008–2009 season was Steve Round who had been assistant to Sam Allardyce during his disastrous spell as Newcastle's manager. This article questioned whether this was really the seminal appointment that we required to break into the top four or whether Moyes and Kenwright had missed a trick.

"A year ago I was looking forward to the new season, seriously believing that Everton could break that glass ceiling and force their way into the top four. Approaching Easter it appeared that the dream might come true. But, one dramatic floodlit night at Goodison, saw us pulverise Fiorentina but still get eliminated from the UEFA Cup and our doubts and injuries multiplied and we limped over the finishing line just ahead of Villa in fifth place in the middle of May. My view twelve months ago was that we just had to keep pace more convincingly with the big four; not over a whole season, but in head to head matches against them, and we would bridge the gap. I pointed out that in the 2006–2007 season we had more than matched the elite four for an hour of most of our contests against them but we had generally faded towards the end of those games. I suggested that, a combination of more nous from Moyes with his substitutions and tactics and a bigger squad, could solve this problem. So, what happened last season? We picked up a record low number of points against the teams we are trying to emulate, but finished as 'champions' of the also-rans by virtue of having a very impressive record against almost everyone else in the Premier League. The sorry tale against the Champions League qualifiers was as follows:

OPPONENT	WON	DREW	LOST	FOR	AGAINST	POINTS
MAN UTD	0	0	2	1	3	0
CHELSEA	0	1	1	1	2	1
ARSENAL	0	0	2	1	5	0
LIVERPOOL	0	0	2	1	3	0
	------------	------------	----------	----------	----------	-------------
TOTAL:	0	1	7	4	13	1

So, but for one of the goals of the season from Tim Cahill deep into injury time after being pretty well beaten out of sight down at Stamford Bridge in November, we would have achieved that score immortalised by Norwegian Eurovision Song Contest entries in the eighties. Add to that, the two defeats in the Mickey Mouse Cup against Chelsea and you can see why we fell well short of that Champions League place at the end of the season. What is most galling, though, is that, if we had replicated our results of the 2006–2007 campaign against the top four last time out, we would have actually finished fourth. We would have gained eight points more and Liverpool would have had five fewer. In the end, though, I'm clutching at straws here, aren't I? Like many Evertonians, I torture myself and console myself in equal measure with such analysis of statistics. I approach every season looking for the most faintly flickering sign that might suggest that this is the year when we can reach the Promised Land of games in the Nou Camp and San Siro. My articles over the past four years have often focused on how we can achieve our rightful place at the high table of European and World football. We all know, through our history and tradition and by the way we try to play the game and our abhorrence of cheating and diving and our shunning of all the bad practices that are infesting modern football, that we should be regarded much more highly around the world than we currently are. Unfortunately, until we start to compete regularly in the Champions League, we will remain one of football's best kept secrets. Apart from drawing solace from statistics, I have looked at other ways that Everton might just reach the Holy Grail; more consistency, an inspirational captain, a greater self-belief and so on.

While many of these points may be valid, I have probably been tinkering around the edges. The problem clearly is, that this conundrum has one extra condition attached to it that makes it so much harder to solve than it might otherwise have been. Unlike Chelsea we cannot 'keep our house in order' as their CEO, Peter Kenyon sermonised to us all. We can only assume that he is referring to the mad economics of Chelsea that allows his club to spend £150 million that it doesn't have on top-of-the-range mercenaries and be pretty unconcerned if they turn out to be crap. While all true football fans around the world would love to see Abramovich, the Glazers and Hicks and Gillette lose interest in a sport that doesn't particularly interest them in the first place and leave Chelsea, Man Utd and Liverpool tumbling into the Gretna graveyard, we all have to accept that it is not something that we can rely on happening in the short term. So, we are left with a puzzle to solve that possibly has no solution other than big financial investment. I would like to think that Everton will not sell its soul to some foreign opportunists with deep pockets and an attention-seeking deficit, but will instead keep in touch with its fans and heritage. Therefore, I am left with this interminable question: How can Everton reach the Champions League without any significant money to speak of? 2004–2005 gives us some hope but our fourth place finish that year did involve heavy dependence on the shower across the park being even more wasteful than normal with their money and more inept on the field than we could ever have dared to dream. Nowadays, we can generally rely on Liverpool being pretty ineffectual but, with Gerrard and Torres, they are always likely to cover up for the mediocrity of the rest of their team and stumble across a reasonable haul of points. No, let's not depend on the inadequacy of the bumbling Spanish waiter, and let's do this for ourselves.

I think that Moyes and Kenwright are right in their transfer policy ("what, sign no one?" I hear you ask). They are determined to focus on one or two key players that will really move us up to a new level. In military terms, we go for surgical strikes in the transfer market rather than blanket bombing, thus minimising the chances of suffering the collateral damage of the past such as finding the likes of Simon Davies on our payroll. David Moyes' record of buying players over the past few years in terms of value for money is second to none; Yakubu, Lescott, Pienaar, Jagielka. The fact that he has managed to get a potential £13 million for AJ shows how he has made the stock of even our relatively ordinary acquisitions rise. I like the fact that he wants to replace AJ with a £20 million Portuguese 21-year-old international. We probably won't land him but the intention to slowly but surely raise the quality of the squad is encouraging. A Sunderland or a Wigan may spend the same money on five or six players but that just shows that we have moved ahead of such teams. One injury free Jaoa Moutinho is worth more than five squad fillers of washed up pros and Norwegian sun-seekers. We are definitely moving in the right direction with our transfer policy. Because of the lack of funds, we will have to sacrifice quantity for quality and pray for few injuries throughout the next ten months, but I still believe that this is the way to go.

At the time of writing, we have actually signed nobody, though. I tell a lie. On 4 July we signed someone called Steve Round. He has replaced Alan Irvine as our assistant manager. I have to confess to being pretty underwhelmed by this particular signing. I don't know the guy and I believe he comes with good credentials but my feeling is that we have missed an opportunity to noticeably progress here. Despite all of Everton's admirable spurning of many of the unwelcome facets of the modern game, believing in traditional above trendy, there is one development of the past decade or so that I believe we should now embrace. I am talking about the foreign coach. The top four are engulfed by them and, as we know, our national association (and Ireland's) believes that its representative team cannot function effectively on the world stage without the ideas and new dimension offered by a foreigner at the helm. I am, probably like most Evertonians, cautious on such matters. Unlike the fickle, fad following Chelsea, a club with a history as fleeting as their managers' contracts, Everton is cautious about anything that may impinge on its famous ancestry. Like a yoke round our neck? Not really, just a club with a history to respect, unlike many others. Our protracted ground move is further evidence of how change is bound to be slow when 130 years of proud tradition is at stake.

The likes of Chelsea and Liverpool are now clubs with no real identity; their supporters hang their colours on a group of foreign stars who couldn't care less what colour shirt they pull on as long as it's worth a hundred grand a week. However, the evidence that there is something to be said for integrating Johnnie Foreigner in to the management structure is there. Ferguson has lamented the loss of Quieroz as his assistant over this summer not least, I suspect, for his communication skills with the likes of Ronaldo and Nani etc. No disrespect to Steve, but I suspect he is unlikely to make Arteta feel any more at home on freezing Merseyside in February than David Moyes has managed. Chelsea didn't even consider looking within the shores of the UK when searching for a replacement for the hapless Israeli undertaker and the other two in the leading quartet also have foreign managers. I wouldn't give the fat Spanish waiter credit for anything, least of all football management, not just because he is manager of the Dark Side but because he is genuinely clueless. The exception does not necessarily disprove the rule, though. The most shining example on which to rest my case is found at the Emirates. One of the most insipid Everton games of last season was one of our most crucial. We needed a point at Arsenal to guarantee fifth place on the 4 of May. Arsenal had just about nothing to play for and had half a team in the stands including the middle of their midfield, Fabregas and Flamini. It was a game there for our taking but we still lost 1–0. Our midfield included Pienaar, Osman and Fernandes; three, what I would consider, Arsenal type players. On paper, you could have argued that our midfield was stronger than theirs on that particular afternoon and yet we still failed to dominate that area of the game. I thought at the time; if the managers had been swapped just for that match, the result would probably have also been switched round. That little bit of subtlety and lateral thinking of the foreign coach on the training ground as well as in the dugout on match days could just elevate some of our very good players into world class players. Steve Round has worked with Steve McLaren, Kevin Keegan and Sam Allardyce. I'm more inclined to shudder than tingle with anticipation at such influences. Are they names that will have helped Steve Round to take us on to the next level? Personally, I don't think so.

So, as I come full circle in the last twelve months and anticipate a new season with the usual foolhardy optimism, I am just a little less sanguine about our coming prospects. I have tried all solutions to give us that edge to finish the season in the top four without having to solve the mother hen of all chicken and egg problems – Champions League football will bring the required financial clout, but Champions League football is unlikely to be achieved without the required monetary muscle. And I can't help but feel, with the introduction of our new assistant manager, the solutions are no nearer. Indeed, I have a funny feeling that we will be going Round in circles for a bit longer yet."

Five years on, I got my wish. Will the classy Martinez bring that new dimension to our coaching? Having spent so many years at Wigan as a player and a manager, he will also appreciate the traditions of an old-fashioned northern, working class environment. It all seems to add up to me.

Chapter 20: Another Kenyon crisis.

(OCTOBER 2008).

In the space of six months we seemed to have gone from having our strongest squad in recent history to our most flimsy. The injury to Yakubu didn't help and we were well off the pace going into the Autumn of 2008. Time to direct my wrath towards other topical football affairs.

"At the start of the year, our TV screens were full of harrowing pictures of mayhem and murder from East Africa. Every news bulletin was saturated with terrible images of, what was to be dubbed, the Kenyan crisis as the two major tribes of that stunning country sought retribution against each other after a rigged election. The stubborn, self-obsessed, myopic, power-crazed leaders had caused this situation to develop. In July another Kenyon, the CEO of Chelsea, showed the same 'qualities' as Odinga and Kibaki when he said that other English football clubs should not moan about his club for sponging off the Abramavich millions, but should simply get their own houses in order, like Chelsea.

In the African Kenyan crisis we saw houses collapsing every day, amidst the carnage. I fear that the Chelsea Kenyon, if obeyed, could lead us to the equivalent destruction of the game of football as we know it in England. To use his own metaphor, if the football industry in England were considered to be a house and it is left in the hands of people like him, then it is in imminent danger of being turned into rubble like some of the towns that suffered in the post-election blood-letting around the Rift Valley.

Peter Kenyon is a dangerous man who now claims that the spiralling debt in football is not the fault of Chelsea. Remembering that his sole motivation in life is the generation of personal wealth and has nothing to do with the well-being of the game, (why else would anyone switch from a high-ranking post at Man Utd to a similar one at Chelsea?) let's look at the kind of house Mr Kenyon and his ilk have constructed for us here in the land of English football.

We'll start at the bottom and look at the foundations. They appear pretty shaky to me. Why have Luton Town, Bournemouth and Rotherham started the season on negative points? Amongst other reasons, they are being punished for going bankrupt. Perhaps we should look more closely at why they have gone bankrupt. They have gone under because they were living beyond their means and much of this is because the likes of Chelsea have created football hyper-inflation. Their ridiculous salaries and transfer fees have dragged everything upwards and naturally this pull effect filters all the way down to the bottom. The teams mentioned above are just the ones that have been caught out so far. Many others are existing on a wing and the prayer that they'll have a good cup run and pull in one of the Premier League giants for a one-off windfall. The fact is, several more clubs will go to the wall this year and the next and they might not suffer just a points deduction; they may disappear completely, like Gretna.

For the small-minded Kenyon, of course, the foundations don't matter. Let the Rochdales and the Swindons of this world dissolve in their own debt. Who cares? In fact, even let the Hulls, Stokes and Wigans vanish. Then Chelsea would be rid of these nuisance matches that get in the way of real games in the Champions League and against 'the big four' (yawn). He must become so anguished that football isn't like other industries. Why can't the big fish just eat the small fry? Let monopolies rule. Survival of the fittest and all that. If Barnsley knock Chelsea out of the FA Cup, then Chelsea should be allowed to simply buy them; Barnsley becomes a subsidiary of Chelsea and the West London mercenaries carry on their merry way to Wembley. The rest of us, though, with an intelligence above that of your average warthog and a vision beyond that of a blind man, will know that foundations are important. A house needs solid foundations in order to stand up.

The football industry needs them to maintain an interest at grassroots level, to provide the lifeblood of communities and, in some cases, to provide the talent for the greedy, egomaniacal Premier League elite. Elaborate scouting networks and plush academies may have considerably reduced the number of 'jewels' being uncovered in Leagues one and two and below, but virtually every professional player developed their initial interest in the game by watching a local team whether it was at a 50,000 all-seater stadium in the upper echelons of the Premier League or the tea bar and perimeter railings of a non-league outfit. The point is, every team matters and plays its part. We don't want to start bailing out clubs with FA hand-outs or nationalising them as seems to be the fad with ailing banks at the moment, but we could perhaps redistribute money in a more socially conscious manner. The breaking away of the self-interested Premier League in 1992 was the root of this gross disparity that now exists in the football food chain. Surely we could now think about healing some of this damage before the football world begins to mirror the real world and implodes in a financial holocaust. A pooling of the resources of all the leagues could be considered and used to redistribute to all members of the football community in a manner that ensures everyone's survival. After all, every team should be considered a valued member of the football family and, if we lose just one team, that should upset us all. To create this pool, there could be some sort of internal tax system, whereby the Premier League teams pay in a proportion of their gate receipts. How about criminalising agents to eliminate them from the game like we're supposed to be doing with ticket touts? All the money currently leaking out of the game into the pockets of these parasites could, instead, be paid into the pool as some sort of stamp duty for all transfer fees over, say, five million. Television money could be distributed more equitably and why not automatically share all gate receipts from cup matches 50:50? After all, it is not a team's fault that it is drawn away. Or perhaps a more sophisticated formula can be devised to work out proportions of gate receipts from cup matches to each participating team on a sliding scale that favours the team from the lower league. Why not... do something, anything, to ensure that the small clubs don't go bust on a regular basis? Not enough thought and effort has been put into the issue of sharing more fairly the massive pot of money generated by football. This is, of course, because the likes of Peter Kenyon do not think it is important.

So, if the foundations are unstable, what about the ceiling? Well, when it comes to salaries, there isn't one! While the clubs in the lower leagues scrabble around with their players making a modest living, the clubs at the top believe the sky's the limit. It is impossible to restrict transfer fees because it's a free market, although the stamp duty might dampen things a little but, what about a wage ceiling? One exists in the football league and it has helped give the weak-willed directors of football clubs a ready-made excuse to the fans for not bankrupting the club on exorbitant wage bills without appearing to be the bad guy. How Leeds Utd must now wish that Peter Ridsdale had not kept saying 'yes' seven years ago simply to please the fans but, instead, been reined in by some sort of financial regulations to curb his populist instincts. There is an argument against the concept of a wage cap that is constantly trotted out and, every time that I hear it, I feel like throwing something large and life-threatening in the direction of the person responsible for making the point. The counter-argument goes, if we restrict the amount that we are allowed to pay our players in England, then the top talent will all leave our shores and go to Spain or Italy or wherever they can earn their telephone number salaries. Immediately, on hearing this drivel, a voice comes in the back of my head saying 'so what?' and then there is silence in my head because, unless you are a supporter of one of the faceless, money drenched franchises like Chelsea, Man Utd or Liverpool, you have nothing to fear. Why do the supporters of all other clubs watch any of these teams play football? I think I represent the true football fanatic, when I say that it is not because we want to see Drogba, Ronaldo or Torres showing off their skills. Quite the reverse; it is because we want to see these players kicked off the park or red-carded and, thus, inadvertently contributing to a rare defeat for their team. If the likes of Drogba, Ronaldo and Torres pissed off to the Mediterranean because their salary was going to be quartered (and such players undoubtedly would leave as they have absolutely no affinity or loyalty towards the clubs for whom they play) would the rest of us shed even one tear? We boast about everyone wanting to come to the Premier League because it's the most competitive league in the world but we are deluding ourselves. It is actually not very competitive at all. Every year Spain, Germany and Italy send at least one different representative to the Champions League from the year before. Bayern Munich and A.C. Milan have ended up in the UEFA Cup in the past two seasons. Since Everton broke the mould in 2005, the top four each year has been the same in England as it was the year before we gate-crashed the party. This season is already shaping up to be a very familiar story. Man City may think that they've got a chance but they, in fact, demonstrate the point I'm making. Only when an even richer billionaire comes into the boardroom, can a club seriously think of upsetting the status quo. Like Formula 1, the winners used to be determined more by finance than ability. But Formula 1 has made some internal adjustments so that the competition is much more a test of the drivers' dexterity than the expertise and money behind the engineering. We now have a very exciting climax to the drivers' championship.

So, the answer is simple; put a ceiling on Premier League wages, let the mercenaries go and bankrupt some other country's league and let us true fans see a real competition, not a predictable procession of the same old soulless superstars parading at the top of the league every season. If European labour laws are an obstacle, find a way to circumvent them as, I believe, the rugby codes did, when they became concerned at the financial outlook of their sport. It takes boldness and courage at the top of the FA and the Premier League which is, no doubt, why it won't happen. Other sports have shown such leadership. Instead we have Scudamore still trying to flog Hull City V Stoke City to the Chinese or Australians as a 39th match. Bold and courageous of a kind, I suppose, but driven by a very confused vision and aimed purely at generating even more money for the richest clubs to further exasperate the problems.

We can now see that the English football house has paper thin foundations and no ceiling. Something I notice every summer, though, is that even the windows are in the wrong place, or, more precisely, are the wrong size. I notice this because I support Everton and almost every year since the windows were put in by FIFA in 2002, Everton have suffered badly from this major design fault. Almost every building needs windows and, in contrast to many football managers, I actually agree with the concept of a transfer window. I like the idea that Everton players are safe from the clutches of the vultures from the rest of Europe for most of the time that the season is in progress. It's stressful enough going through every January and summer wondering whether someone will lure Arteta to Spain or Yobo to London with the brandishing of a chequebook, but I don't think that I could cope with this uncertainty throughout the whole year anymore, especially now that the ruling allowing players to buy out the remainder of their contracts means that long term deals literally are not worth the paper they're written on. At least there is some feeling of comfort in the knowledge that the race for the Premier League starts from an unequivocal position. Everyone knows where they stand. Everyone knows what tools they have to do the job at least until half way through the race when some emergency adjustments can be made before the race continues to the finishing line, again with a fixed payroll. But, actually, this isn't the case. The football house has two windows, a small one and a large one. The large window has been positioned so that it ends at least two weeks after the season has started. This means that the first two or three matches are still experimental and the personnel used may bear little relation to that used for the rest of the campaign. Unless you have so much money like Chelsea who will spend whatever it takes to land their man, the rest of us who support more mortal teams are left to wait to see which teams and players are close enough to tipping point, as the window is closing, to agree to a move. It becomes an exercise in brinkmanship combined with panic. At Everton we remember 2003 when we captured Jeffers, Kilbane, McFadden and Martyn all on deadline day. Apart from Nigel Martyn, none were outstanding successes and we finished fourth from bottom that season. Spudhead's departure on deadline day 2004 didn't disrupt us as much as it might have done mainly because he was already injured and Moyes had clearly worked on the assumption that he was not part of his plans, anyway, but it could have caused serious damage to our prospects, if our season had been planned around our errant prodigy. The Yak's arrival last season came after we'd already dropped four points away to Reading and at home to Blackburn, and he took a month to settle after his transfer. This season has, without doubt, been the worst. Seven kids in the squad and no new signings by the time the first game arrived. Since then, the new faces look promising but, clearly we're using up the first two months of the season bedding them in. As it was a year ago, it may be November before we find consistency which turned out to be the difference between fourth and fifth place at the end of the season. If the whole point of the window is to allow coaches and managers some peace of mind over their squads and a clear idea of what they have to work with, wouldn't it make sense to make the window end, say, a month before the season starts? If players could only be bought and sold for exactly a two month period starting from the last day of the season, all transfer business could be done and dusted by mid-July and managers could work with their known players through most of the pre-season friendlies and build clear strategies, tactics and plans for the coming season. As it is, the first three matches of the league campaign have the manager with one ear on the phone to various agents, one eye on the club's bank balance and not a lot of attention left for what is happening on the pitch. That's certainly the feeling I had watching our first three games against Blackburn, West Brom and Portsmouth. The transfer window was imposed by FIFA but, before it existed, some countries had already put in their own windows, so there's nothing to stop us putting in our own window of the size that suits us. FIFA would probably follow suit, anyway, once they saw how much sense it made. If it disadvantages English teams compared to our continental counterparts, so be it. As with the salary cap, if it means our rich elite miss out on some of the Galacticos flaunting themselves to the highest bidder, will most of us really care? If it again adds to the Premier League becoming a more egalitarian society, then most of us will embrace it.

So, Mr Kenyon, you carry on building your Chelsea castle in the sky and keep sucking up to the Russian dork to keep your life support turned on but let the rest of us live in the real world and try and build a house to last by reinforcing the foundations, putting in a ceiling and making the summer window let in less light. If we don't, we might eventually find all the walls come tumbling down. If we do, then there's hope that the house of English football may just withstand the turmoil of the current global financial climate and, just as importantly, it will be built on a level playing field."

If you think that is angry, just take a look at the next chapter!

Chapter 21: Anger management.

(JANUARY 2009).

The wait for silverware was becoming unbearable. Seven years under Moyes and just the League Cup semi-final defeat to Chelsea twelve months earlier to reflect on, as the closest we'd come to tangible success. Memories of 1984, 1985, 1987 and 1995 were burning like a branding iron in my brain. I needed that feeling back; to be associated with a club that could justifiably claim to be better than all the rest in a particular competition just for one year. I was tired of consoling myself with the knowledge that Everton is the best club in all other respects; we had to prove it on the pitch.

"Perhaps it's due to a marinated brain from the New Year excesses, but there has been little cohesion in my train of thought since we entered 2009. As usual the train that transports my thoughts has generally been heading in the direction of football. Maybe the odd diversion here and there towards the forthcoming school term and the responsibility incumbent upon myself to make sure it's a reasonably successful one for the establishment that I head, but overall the train meanders along a track destined for the next round of key matches which, for Everton, means Hull City at home next Saturday. As we begin a new year, my head is full of questions:

(1) If luck really does even out over the course of a season as everyone always says it does, will Aston Villa manage to scrape into the top half of the table at the end of the season?

(2) If the court case goes the way we all hope it does, how will Liverpool cope with half their team (Steven Gerrard) being in jail. Hopefully the other half (Torres) will be sidelined with a broken finger nail or mascara in the eye and then they'll be completely knackered.

(3) Why didn't Phil Dowd appear in the New Year's honours list under the heading 'services to sport' for actually having the courage to stand up to Chelsea even to the point of taking the piss out of Michael Bollox for questioning his interpretation of ten yards? You can see the festive excesses really have addled my neural network; I didn't think I would ever recommend Phil Dowd for anything other than immediate retirement.

(4) When will Man Utd finally realise that the persecution complex exhibited by their leader (even the fixture list is stacked against his despicable club, apparently) added to his seething anger at virtually everything, is actually a sure sign of the onset of senility and, finally try to restore some dignity to their club, by sacking him? Or, are they going to 'do a Zimbabwe' and allow his institution and all its supporters to become an international symbol of injustice and megalomaniacal dysfunction by letting him cling to his decrepit power just like Mugabe?

The final question that has been spinning in unison with the swirl of my various hangovers is why don't we just forget about the respect campaign imposed at the beginning of this season, given that a significant minority of players, notably Spudhead, are exempt from its enforcement, anyway? I caught a few seconds of an ice hockey match the other day. As usual, there was the mandatory mass punch-up with the hapless match official looking on impotently lest he received a blade in his skull. I presume the offenders were dispatched to the sin-bin, although it would have had to be a skip, to accommodate all the brawlers involved. How they managed to play two-a-side hockey for the next ten minutes, I have no idea. This gratuitous violence seems to be an accepted part of the game. Rugby is only slightly less feral and yet, in both these two sports, does the violence ever translate itself to the spectators? Football supporters are probably a different breed and would fight over a loose remark made about someone's budgie but, as I will explain in a moment, the irrationality of the football hooligan actually supports the argument that we might as well stop trying to encourage good behaviour on the football pitch. This contradicts much of what I have advocated over the past four years but I am fed up with the two tier set of rules that are applied. The idea of football providing good role models has failed. Young kids who follow the Premier League will continue to believe that it is OK to dive because Ronaldo and Drogba and Gerrard do it and are, not just condoned for it, but are actually rewarded. Kids know that Spudhead ejaculates phlegm filled abuse in the faces of referees and it is merely shrugged off by the authorities and justified by his senescent manager while David Moyes naively continues to try to adhere to the respect agenda. Seeing cheating with impunity week in and week out causes most of us to become incandescent with rage, anyway. If anything is going to push me to shed my mild manners and use my fists to ease my anguish, it is seeing cheats like Ronaldo and Rooney getting away with it yet again. If such instant retribution took place on the field of play, though, by, for example, the offending defender giving Ronaldo a good kicking while he's pretending to be injured or a few punches being thrown in the direction of the big ugly Spudhead, I would probably feel a lot less inclined to smack the Man Utd fan standing next to me. How he would react, I cannot legislate for, of course. The moronic majority of Man Utd fans would probably use their fists whatever was transpiring on the pitch, anyway. I, however, would definitely feel some cathartic release by witnessing such vicarious aggression being meted out on the pitch. By all means, issue some short-term punishment like a sin-bin and give red cards with the accompanying bans for the most serious offences but forget about all the drawn out procrastination of the FA investigations, frivolous appeals and fines that players notice about as much as a flea bite. Instant justice on the pitch would be the ideal antidote for much of my pent-up wrath.

This may amount to a U-turn of monumental proportions on my part, but I think it would alleviate my blood pressure significantly, if I saw a bit of vigilantism taking place on the pitch against the cheats of the modern day game. I have watched several matches from the past decade or so over the Christmas period in a TV series of 'A *hundred Greatest Premier League matches'*. Even as recently as eight years ago, referees allowed much more to go in terms of retaliation and raised hands. There was no screeching of indignation from the commentators and fewer red cards; just an acceptance that it's a man's game played by some angry young men.

As you can probably tell from this article, I am becoming a pretty angry man, myself. Perhaps I need to calm down. According to my mum, I was a very angry baby. I screamed every night for the first eighteen months of my life. She never worked it out. I think I have. I was born in 1961. It was towards the end of Everton's longest barren period in terms of trophies. The season before World War Two began, we had won the league. Similar to the fall-out from Heysel, events in Europe outside our control meant we were not able to build on that success. Even if we take 1946 as the year that we relinquished our title, it was still 16 years since we had won anything. In 1963 Harry Catterick's team finally put us back where we belonged at the top of the league. Around that time, my mum stopped having sleepless nights. For much of my early years, I am told I had an aversion to the colour red; I wouldn't eat tomatoes, strawberries, jam etc etc. It was only in 1970 that the true meaning of all this sub-conscious behavioural quirkiness came to light: I was allowed to stay up late for the first time in my life to watch 'Match of the Day' on a Saturday night. The main game was Everton 1 Wolves 0. It was a black and white television so even then I had no idea that Everton were playing in blue, but I decided instantly that Everton was my team and Joe Royle was my idol. Almost immediately after this life-changing decision, I deteriorated into my angry ways again and, by my teens, I was becoming quite morose and uncommunicative. Pubescent twangs? No; Everton went another four-teen years without winning anything. The mid-eighties were joyous times. I lost my first serious girlfriend and aborted my first serious career but Everton were winning everything. Such was my sanguine mood that I stopped hating the red side to the same extent that I had always previously done (although, the tide of hatred did come rushing back when they stole the double off us in 1986). Pickings have been thin ever since. And now, once again, we have reached that fourteen year watershed and, once again, I am becoming very angry indeed as demonstrated in the first few paragraphs of this piece. In my lifetime, I have never gone more than fourteen years without Everton silver-ware. I don't know what might happen if I go beyond that time. Can my heart and body stand such strain with my blood pressure rising faster than property insurance in Gaza? I'm well into middle age; I'm a bit scared of the unknown. I don't need a doctor or a shrink. I don't need counselling, I don't need anger management therapy. I probably don't even need Ferguson to stop practising his angry management despite what I said earlier; I just desperately need Everton to win the FA Cup this year. David Moyes, please help me!"

And he almost did. Once again, though, despite Louis Saha scoring the fastest FA Cup Final goal in history, Tony Hibbert chose Wembley for his worst ever game in an Everton shirt and we fell at the hands of our nemesis, Chelsea, in the showpiece game of the 2008–2009 season.

Chapter 22: The travelling is better than the arriving.

(APRIL 2009).

And as the semi-final against Man Utd approached, nerves had set in and I was already buttressing myself against inevitable disappointment and convincing myself that the Everton way of achieving success may be slow and painstaking, but was ultimately much more fulfilling.

"I've just received issue number 102 of *SFTH*. It takes a while to get to Uganda. As the Yak will tell you, it's not always easy getting across this continent. The first thing I always look at when the fanzine arrives, is the deadline for submissions for the next edition. I have to say that, this time I am dismayed. Our wonderful editor has decided to have issue number 103 on sale the week after the semi-final and so the deadline for items to arrive on his laptop is 16 April i.e. three days *before* the biggest game we've had for 14 years. What's my problem? you may well be asking and so, probably, is the editor. Well, we contributors to this estimable publication don't know what to write about. We are hamstrung by the fact that we can't really talk about what will, no doubt, be the most important thing on the minds of all Evertonians as they read this and all other articles in issue No 103. Do we risk guessing what may have transpired at Wembley last week and, either be hailed as some sort of incredible prophet of great tidings, or have egg on our faces for evermore for predicting the ridiculous, or, indeed be regarded as depressing doom mongers irrespective of whether our forecast of defeat at the hands of Man Utd comes true or not? And, for those of us who are superstitious, the very act of putting into print our attempt to foresee a future result that will actually be set in the concrete of history by the time everyone reads it, is something we cannot bring ourselves to do. The one sure way of Everton losing is for me to bet on them winning but, at the same time, to take the pessimistic view in judging the outcome of 19 April at Wembley, would consume me with feelings of betrayal of my own team. If they were then to lose, I would feel that I had somehow contributed to their downfall. Confused? Well, that's how the adrenalin twists our minds at such pivotal moments in our history. FA Cup semi-finals might not mean much to the supporters of Man Utd or Chelsea, but to us, they are like our wedding day or some audition for a big break in Hollywood. It's unlikely to come around again any time soon and we've got to make sure we cover all bases to make it go the way we want it to. Creating the potential for disastrous auguries by making outrageously optimistic or depressingly pessimistic forecasts about the outcome of our FA Cup last four game against Man Utd, is something to be avoided.

This concludes my prolix explanation as to what I will *not* write about in this article. So, what will I write about? Well, let's talk about certainties, shall we? On 25 April when the Everton players trot out onto the Goodison turf with *The Z Cars* theme ringing in their ears, there is one thing that is an absolute cast iron certainty. That incontrovertible, stonewall foregone conclusion, is that you and I will still support Everton and, more significantly, irrespective of the result from north London last weekend, we will still be very glad that we do not support Man Utd. On the face of it, we may appear to be irrational and illogical human beings. Man Utd have more money, a bigger stadium, better players and a virtual guarantee of silverware every season. They are feted by the media and have masses of supporters all over the world. Some may think we are delusional or simply brain-damaged to persist with our apparently futile allegiance to Everton.

For some of us, of course, it is geographical reasons that forced the decision out of our hands. Being born in the Merseyside region and probably with Evertonian parents, it really was a no-brainer. For others like me, though, I had no such birthright. I was born over 200 miles from the hallowed arena of Goodison Park. My nearest First Division team when I was growing up was Southampton. Virtually all my friends at school supported Leeds United, one of the big London clubs or The Saints (ooh-ahh!). There was one Ipswich Town fan but that was because he was a cousin of Brian Talbot and so had free tickets to all their matches. I, on the other hand, chose to plough a lone furrow, not because of any family connection but because I was never one to follow the crowd and I actually saw something in Everton that, evidently, none of my friends could identify with. My interest in football arrived just in time to catch the coat-tails of the 1969–1970 season and I instantly adored the likes of Kendall, Ball and Harvey and, most notably, Joe Royle.

Many of my friends lost interest in football as they progressed through secondary school. Girls, alcohol and punk rock all began to replace the Subbuteo and the Soccer Stars swaps parties. The graph of their soccer supporting passion began to tail off while mine skyrocketed to a peak at around 13 years old and has never come down since. Knowing that I was probably the only Evertonian in the whole of Andover, developed a trench mentality in me and may explain why, for example, I got into a fight when someone taunted me by calling Bob Latchford a pudding after we had lost the 1977 League Cup Final. So, what is it about Everton that has this effect on people? Evertonians I meet all over the world seem to have a passion and knowledge about their club greater than all other fans. We constantly hear of players who had careers with many different clubs but pick out Everton as being 'special'. A good friend of mine has been a Man Utd season ticket holder for the past forty odd years. He announced at Christmas that he would not renew his season ticket next year. "I'm not completely fed up with it but the excitement is not what it used to be," he lamented in his email. He's 51 and perhaps just going through changes but I can't imagine my enthusiasm for Everton dying like that.

I believe that part of the uniqueness of Everton is that we are a perfect balance between a 'big' club and yet still somehow in touch with the fans. The administration may let the fans down big time with ticket allocation cock-ups and so on, but I still understand where Moyes was coming from when he coined the 'People's Club' sobriquet. We're not quite at the 'going to the game on the bus with Dixie Dean' level as such intimacy with the players will never ever happen again, but we do have a lot of honest, fallible players like Phil Neville and Tony Hibbert who we can identify with, perhaps, partly because we think they do not play football much better than we can, but also because they come across as being as committed to the Everton cause as the supporters. We have a camaraderie in the squad that almost makes us, as fans, feel a part of it. And, I don't believe this is an accident of the present time. The fact that our all-conquering team of the mid-eighties was always referred to as 'the team of no stars' shows that, even when we were playing football from a different planet, we were still somehow down-to-earth. I may be looking through blue-tinted glasses here, but I actually believe that the travelling is better than the arriving. Watching a bunch of players every week slowly but surely getting better and tantalisingly closing the gap on the top four, is more fulfilling than seeing your team buy success and then being disappointed when the fourth trophy of the season slips from your grasp meaning you have to make do with a paltry three. The football spectacle for Man Utd followers may be exhilarating at times but, the fact that it's served up by people who have not an ounce of humility or, indeed, understanding of the people who pay to watch them, makes them detached and distant and ultimately worthless. The love of the club that binds the supporters is not shared or even cognized by your average Man Utd or Chelsea or Liverpool player who would leave at the whiff of a wad of Spanish or Italian euros without even a cursory glance over the shoulder, if the wad were bigger than the one they currently earned. Rooney did it to us once, but Moyes has been careful not to involve himself with such mercenaries ever since. The managers and owners of these megabucks clubs also reciprocate this shallow disregard for the human aspect of the industry that most fans crave. Chelsea and Liverpool superstars, in particular, are bought and then tossed away with the caprice and frequency of mobile phones. They are truly the ultimate example of our disposable society. How many Liverpool fans were pleased to see Keane lying in the Anfield garbage after less than six months? Many, I suspect wanted to rescue him and take him straight back to Benitez to give him another try; but football fans have no such say in the matters of their own club.

That is why true Man Utd fans like my friend, Steve, are becoming disillusioned and bored with it all. Most of the 70,000 that fill Old Trafford every week are not from his generation of Charlton, Best and Law and are not true Man Utd fans. They are carted to the ground each week on their huge bandwagon, intoxicated by the thought of success with no second thought for how it is achieved. They haven't the patience for the sweat and effort that can go into a genuine achievement. They want the success that is achieved by buying Berbatov or Rooney on deadline day, thus hoping to have the double effect of screwing up another club's season, as well as enhancing their own. True, they then have a certain guarantee of seeing exciting, winning football but it stops there; it is shallow and short-lived. Man Utd fans are bought a brand new Ferrari every year but we, at Everton get much more pleasure from our reliable BMW that we have taken years to save up for. The majority of the people who occupy Old Trafford every week are supporters of football. Week in and week out, Goodison is packed with football supporters. There is a subtle but very significant difference. There is no room for prawn sandwiches when you watch Everton.

I am now going to make a very controversial statement. I do not think that our squad is too small! Let me explain. If everyone was fit, we could name an eighteen of:

Howard, Nash, Hibbert, Jacobsen, Jagielka, Yobo, Lescott, Baines, Osman, Arteta, Neville, Fellaini, Pienaar, Gosling, Rodwell, Cahill, Saha, Yakubu.

I've left out Van de Meyde, Valente, Anichebe, Vaughan, Castillo, Jo and a handful of promising youngsters.

Sorry to show my age again, but I'm going to harp on about the past once more. In our most successful season ever of 1984–1985 we played 63 matches but, until we put out a reserve team for the last three matches when the league was won, we used a total of eighteen players i.e. a modern day Saturday afternoon team sheet (including substitutes). Contrary to the rubbish churned out by Harry Redknapp, there *were* European matches played three days before domestic Cup Finals in the 'old days'. In 1985 Everton put out their strongest team for both and unfortunately lost the FA Cup to Man Utd three days after winning the Cup Winners Cup final. In those days, there was no such thing as an 'international break'. There were 42 league games and just twelve players were named for each match. I remember I used to always feel sorry for either Alan Harper or Kevin Richardson who, invariably, were the unlucky 'thirteenth man' each week. That, though, illustrates the point I'm making; I actually felt a sort of empathy for the players who represented the Blues or who narrowly missed out. We had such a regular first eleven that they all had their own individual song that would emanate from the Gwladys Street before each home game and would fade with a cheer and a round of applause as each player acknowledged his own particular signature tune. The game has become faster and tougher and injuries are more likely but, assuming this season has been exceptionally unlucky in terms of long term lay-offs, a first team squad of 33, which is what we now have, is still more than enough, I believe. By concentrating on about half of those, though, it allows the fans to remain familiar with their players, get to know their idiosyncrasies and annoying frailties and feel that we are somehow connected. I'm not naïve enough to believe everything that I read in the press, but it is good to hear that no amount of money would tempt Tim Cahill to play for Liverpool or that captaining Everton is the proudest honour that Phil Neville has ever achieved in the game or that Mikel Arteta is a man of his word and genuinely loves Everton. No doubt there will be a disappointment or two in the future (especially as we become more successful) although, to be fair, since Rooney left, there has not been a single regrettable departure from the 'School of Science'. The fact that Jo seems to have found a home with us and the likes of Hibbert and Osman could become one club players (when was the last time that happened at Everton?) shows that there is a stability and consistency about our squad that most other Premier League teams must envy. An intimate, slowly evolving squad means there is time for us to get to know any new signings like family members and for them to get to love the blue shirt. And, very gradually, the quality will increase as each addition to the squad is an improvement on the one being replaced. I'm sure Moyes has assessed the mentality as much as the talent of players like Moutinho. He knows that another Rooney could unbalance the whole delicate equilibrium of the changing room and unravel years of painstaking team building. So, I hope that Moyes will continue to favour work ethic over ego when recruiting new players and I hope that we will not get a sugar-daddy to come throwing his billions around to change the whole fabric of our club. I actually hope that our squad is not changed too drastically in the summer but just gently tweaked here and there. I don't want Moyes to indulge in squad rotation or wage battles with prima donnas, but let's keep the team in touch with the people that support it. Let's keep our squad paper thin and continue to defy the odds and eventually our thin blue line may just make it all the way to the summit and, when it does, we may also find that the air there a lot sweeter than it is for Man Utd or Chelsea fans who never enjoyed (or endured?) the climb to get there in the first place."

And the wait went on...

Chapter 23: Thank you, Rooney... for leaving.

(AUGUST 2009).

And here's another essay to convince Evertonians that Champions League football and silverware were not all that mattered, and we did have things to celebrate; like the five year anniversary of the departure of the Fat One.

"There ought to be a law against, anyone who takes offence, in a day in his celebration..."

Unusual to start a *SFTH* article with the opening lines of a Stevie Wonder 1981 hit but I think it is fitting on this occasion. We are fast approaching the fifth anniversary of a turning point in the history of Everton Football Club. At the time, many thought it was a point when we turned backwards, a point when the club showed that it had finally given up the fight to be part of the football high table and had admitted that it no longer had the financial muscle to live with the big boys. A point in time when we would concede forevermore that our rich tradition that is longer and more illustrious than any other club on the planet, counted for nothing in the new world order of instant money-injected gratification. On that day half a decade ago, our club was actually indulging in a quick financial fix of its own, but that was, according to some sources at the time, an infusion of cash required merely to stay alive. I am, of course, referring to the day that a certain Wayne Rooney departed for the yonder fields of all that is depressingly bad in modern day football. We will all recall that it was many months earlier that our once beloved Spudface had played his last game for us. He played in an ignominious 5–1 defeat to Man City (a club that inhabited our own mortal world in those days) as we struggled to keep our chins above the relegation cord. He then swanned off to play for England in Euro 2004, snapped his metatarsal and, as far as Evertonians were concerned, he was history.

At that point, five years ago, I took a rather different path to many fellow Blues. Perhaps blurred by my distance from the action or from too much African sun frying my brain, I saw this as a turning point in the *right* direction for our club. My writing career with this fanzine was launched accordingly. My gut feeling was that Everton is a club with such a powerful and honourable history, that we should never sell out to the smutty, unprincipled people that inhabit the world of football these days. Rooney was a prime example of the cocky, self-interested, obnoxious professional footballer of the 21st-century marque. At eighteen he was already transfixed with pound signs in his eyes and the belief that his footballing ability was something that the whole world masturbated over. He simply lost touch with reality and there was only one destination; the unreal, showbiz goldfish bowl of a club like Man Utd. He hasn't handled it particularly well; he still has his adolescent tantrums on the pitch and gets in the occasional embarrassing scrapes off it, but this is inevitable. As they say in Africa; "You can take the kid out of the village, but you can never take the village out of the kid." None of it matters to either Rooney or Man Utd, though, as they have accepted that this is the price to pay for success in the modern celebrity-driven world. I sometimes wonder what is going through Bobby Charlton's mind when he's interviewed and he tries to cling on to some distant memories of the sepia tinted days when he was a player and Man Utd still had dignity and attracted genuine affection. Deep down, he probably wishes that he had been shackled inextricably to a club like Everton that has shunned the more shallow aspects of the modern era. Instead, he has to reluctantly accept his association with the glutinous, ugly world of his Red Devils.

David Moyes, perhaps not entirely by choice, has also shunned the parallel universe that the likes of Real Madrid, Man Utd and Chelsea exist in. He would no doubt like a lot more to spend but does he really envy someone like Mark Hughes? Firstly, the pressure on him to deliver a trophy quickly at Money City must be almost debilitating. Secondly, isn't part of the skill of management being able to use limited resources effectively? Turning Arteta into one of the Premier League's most coveted players or quadrupling the value of Lescott in three years must add more to your self-esteem, not to mention your CV, than the purchase of established world beaters to make up a successful team. I still contend that Mourinho's record in destroying recognised talent, eg Duff, Shevchenko, Wright-Phillips, Parker, Kezman, Mutu etc etc far outweighs the achievements he may claim is evident in the silverware he collected in his three years at Chelsea. There is little doubt that Moyes still has a belief in some old-fashioned values; integrity, honesty and loyalty. Just as Brian Clough found when he tried to massage some down to earth virtues into the pampered egos of the Leeds United superstars 35 years ago and lasted 44 days, I am sure Moyes would suffer the same fate if he tried to apply his methods at Man Utd where so many 'experts' think he will end up. For a start, he would have to reacquaint himself with the potato-headed brat.

Moyes and Rooney are from different ends of the evolutionary scale when it comes to being a decent human being. Everton was not big enough for the both of them. I, for one, am so glad that it was Moyes who stayed. And that is why I wish to propose that all Evertonians treat 31 August as a day of celebration in the club's history. Perhaps the blue half (sorry, nine tenths) of Liverpool could even take it as a national holiday every year from now on. In fact, every Evertonian, anywhere in the world, should be entitled to one day's paid leave on that day when we have barbecues and street parties and firework displays and we play the *Z-Cars* theme loudly and sing *"It's a grand old team"* in parks and city centres around the globe. And we call it World Blue Day, but we don't mention the name Rooney, even though we have him to thank for it, because we don't want to fertilise his already overblown ego any further. And, as the sun sets on World Blue Day, we reminisce over our beers and champagne on how Everton's fortunes improved spectacularly from 31 August 2005 when we were relegation certainties, but ended up in the Champions League nine months later. We will talk about the consistent European qualification ever since and how that FA Cup Final of 2009 was just the beginning of years of glory, both at home and abroad, all achieved without caving in to the mercenaries and bloodsuckers that feature in the modern game, that are so far removed from the real people who make it all work; the fans.

And, when the prodigal son takes an envious look over his shoulder in the twilight of his career, and when the self-abusive life style starts to cause the inevitable decline and, like the spoilt little child he is, he decides he would like to return to his so-called spiritual home, we just smile and tell him that this is a private party and our days of signing washed-up faded glitter like Ginola and Gazza are over. In fact, those days were over from the second that David Moyes entered the doors of Goodison with his new meritocracy. If you don't pull your weight, you're out. If you have no moral stature, you're out.

So, Wayne… Warren, whatever your name is, we don't really care, you should realise that, when you jumped on the gravy train five years ago, you cut all ties with the real world of true football fans and we have done much better without you, thank you very much and, if you feel a twinge of sadness over this fact, you may just recall a song from your childhood, if your limited memory span can extend back that far. It went something (but not exactly) like this, but this is how you should remember it:

'When you know you're history, it's enough to make your heart go low, low, low. They don't care what the fat spud said, what the fuck do they care. Cos' they only know that there's gonna be a show when the Everton boys are there.'"

And how Moyes and Rooney work together (if, indeed, Moyes keeps him at United) remains the most intriguing question in football as we approach the 2013–2014 season.

Chapter 24: Déjà vu.

(NOVEMBER 2009).

Things were once again looking bleak at the start of the 2009–2010 season. In fact, it seemed that we had been here before.

"So, there I am, in the bar relaxing in my chair with a cold Club beer in my right hand and West Ham V Everton is just about to unfold in front of me on the big flat screen. The final notes of 'Happy Birthday' have just subsided as my daughter, Clair's excited gaggle of friends gradually disburse clutching a 'party bag' of goodies in the care of a parent or two. After 27 minutes of mediocre, breathless football on, what always appears on TV to be a very cramped Upton Park, out of nothing King Louie produces a piece of magic from outside the penalty area with his left foot and Everton have an underserved lead. And I have to pinch myself; not because I can't believe we have scored, although it has to be said it was pretty unexpected and seemed extremely unlikely at the time it happened, but because I've seen it all before. Let me take you back 12 months to exactly the same time on exactly the same day:

So, there I was, in the bar relaxing in my chair with a cold Club beer in my right hand and West Ham V Everton was just about to unfold in front of me on the small curved screen (so the TV has improved in the past year). The final notes of 'Happy Birthday' had just subsided as my daughter, Clair's excited gaggle of friends gradually disbursed clutching a 'party bag' of goodies in the care of a parent or two. After 84 minutes of mediocre, breathless football on the cramped Upton Park, out of nothing King Louie produced a piece of magic from outside of the penalty area with his left foot and Everton had an undeserved lead.

So, let's spot the similarities and differences. The date (8 November) and the time of kick-off (3.00 p.m. (6.00 p.m. in Uganda)) are identical. The opposition and venue are the same and our start to the season is almost identical; before the game in 2008 we had 15 points from 10 games having won four, drawn three and lost four. Because of Europa League commitments, we had played one less game this time but the win against West Ham meant that we had a record of, yes, won 4, drawn 3 and lost 4. We were struggling to find rhythm a year ago as the transfer window had crashed into the start of our campaign with a crop of deadline week signings still settling in. This season we've had a slow start because we had a crop of deadline signings still... yes, see what I mean? Saha's goal in 2008 gave us a 2–1 lead not a one-nil lead as Elephant Man had just equalised for us a couple of minutes earlier but, all in all, the similarities are uncanny. Even the attendance was more or less the same, 32,466 in 2007 compared with 33,961 twelve months earlier. Clair's age, of course, increased by one; from five to six.

So where is all this leading? Not very far, really. Except that it made me think how everything is becoming so very familiar; like I've seen it all before. It's appropriate that a Frenchman is the central figure in the above tale of replication, because it is a stolen piece of his language that springs to mind at this juncture; déjà-vu. Directly translated it means 'already seen' and the way this season has transpired, everything is really beginning to seem very much like we've all been here before.

Later that day, Man Utd lost. Sadly not a very familiar occurrence but the reaction of their sour-spirited manager at the end was definitely something that we have all heard many times before. There we were, believing that Man Utd had come second best in a genuine duel of two teams competing at the highest level but, no, we were all wrong, weren't we? The knighted geriatric tells us it was actually, yet again, the referee who beat Man Utd. And his nauseating disciples who, we are told, have all lost faith in all the referees, concur and one of them even gets rewarded with the England captaincy for yet another display of immaturity that I would not allow from Clair, let alone someone who has just become a father for the first time (scary isn't it?). All so tiresome, all so, well, déjà-vu. And in that Chelsea V United match, we saw a big 14 stone figure of muscle and athleticism rolling around like a floundering fish searching for water when he was challenged near the end of the game. We quickly do a scour of the fixtures for the interminable international break coming up and, sure enough, Ivory Coast have a meaningless match the following weekend; certainly a match that a pampered £130,000 a week ego need not dirty his shirt for. Did anyone hear any more about Drogba's apparently life-threatening injury after that kick in the ribs from Jonny Evans? Of course not and, of course, Chelsea are too scared of upsetting their black diamond to say anything derogatory in his direction. As a result, their club is further embarrassed and their reputation falls further into the mire of selling out to this crass cheating and manipulation. But, hey, they keep winning and their moronic fans are satisfied so, what the hell.

And the week progressed and we find that Man Utd are sniffing around more of our young talent that we have worked so hard to nurture and will lure Rodwell with promises of untold riches. Surely Rodwell is made of stronger fibre, though. I mean he has GCSE's, doesn't he? Rooney couldn't even spell GCSE!

And then I notice on Sky News, their schedule of live matches and I see that Everton have apparently disappeared from their radar for almost an entire two months between 6 December and 27 January and that same old sinking feeling comes over me again. Outside the 'Big Fat Boring Four' Everton have been 'champions' for the past two seasons and yet, for seven weeks when the Premier League programme is at its most congested, we effectively don't even exist according to Sky. It doesn't affect me because all our games are shown, either live or recorded, here in Uganda, but it's a principle that leaves me incandescent. And, hang on, did I say that every single game can be seen here? Actually, of the 117 Premier League games so far completed this season, one solitary one was not shown. On 25 October Bolton V Everton was not shown at all either live or recorded by our satellite provider. To watch Everton at home to Wolves or Everton at home to Villa, we diehard fans have had to stay up until three o'clock on a Sunday morning. Just as Sky surmise with the British populace that no one likes Everton, DSTV assume that no one on the African continent is interested in the club from Merseyside with a history that Man Utd can only dream of. They almost blacked out the FA Cup Final because they thought no one would be interested in a final that did not involve Arsenal, Man Utd or Liverpool. Bizarrely, supporters on this continent who support Hull City or Burnley are afforded much greater deference and consideration than supporters of Everton, by the sole provider of live international football transmitted from South Africa. It's a disgrace and it's an insult to the intelligent people who pay their $120 subscription expecting a balanced coverage of the English Premier League.

And the old chestnuts keep rolling out for Evertonians; why do Everton have a fallibility to knee injuries? Why is it, when The Dark Side are having a nightmare, we always seem to be having a slightly worse one? And why is David Moyes the only manager who is big enough to accept referee decisions and to act with dignity in defeat just like most Everton managers before him? It's all so recurrent, so damned repetitious, so bloody déjà-vu.

So, where do we go from here? Do we give up, accept the status quo, support our team against the odds and accept that the world of professional football is now set in such solid stone that we can forget about any hope of change? The night following our take-two at the Anne Boleyn postage stamp of a ground, Liverpool also did a very familiar thing; they drew at home to probable relegation fodder and needed some blatant cheating to reach even that modest achievement. Déjà-vu? Of course, but maybe this time they have taken it all a little too far. Six defeats in eight, the manager even more clueless than ever, and even less bothered about whether the team he manages wins or loses. (Why was he the only one present at Anfield on that Sunday to show not a smidgeon of emotion when his awful team beat Man Utd?). But, with Statler and Waldorf (remember the Muppets?) still squabbling in the best seats, there is more chance of Owen playing for England again, than Benitez being sacked. As was mentioned earlier, at the time of writing, Everton have an identical record to this time last year. We have a crop of long-term injured to return before Christmas, so, surely we can achieve at least the 63 points we achieved last year. Even now, we are just four points off fourth place, if we win our game in hand. Villa are no better than last year. Man City will be lucky to finish in the top half with their comical defending. Tottenham are our biggest threat and our results against them could be crucial. As for the team that holds the key to Number four at the moment i.e. the only member of the 'Big Hideous Tedious Four' not currently in the top three, the team that was defeated and deflated by a beach ball (did Reina mistake it for Scummy Lee, by the way?), they look extremely shaky. In 2005, 61 points was sufficient for us to qualify for the Champions' League, partly because Liverpool were so dire. Surely next May we can once again be calling the ham-fisted Spanish half-wit, Mr Beneathus, and we can once again break the mould and proudly strut on the big stage, just like four years ago. Now that would be a very sweet déjà-vu indeed."

A further rant about the unbalanced coverage of Everton from the main satellite television provider for sub-Saharan Africa appeared in *SFTH* soon afterwards. It probably said more about my personal state of mind, than any deliberate conspiracy on the part of DSTV and it appears in Chapter 29 of *Expat Evertonian*.

Chapter 25: Professionalism versus Passion – why England will never win anything.

(JANUARY 2010).

2010 was a year that held more significance than all previous years for football fans on the continent on which I resided at that time. For the first time ever, Africa would provide the very soil on which the World Cup would be contested. My anticipation perversely was as much towards seeing England fail as it was towards seeing the games played amidst the colour of the Rainbow Nation and the cacophony of the vuvuzelas.

"I've decided to be a serious writer. No more of this emotive fanspeak; let's have a reasoned debate in sensible unemotional language presented in considered, balanced prose with none of the insulting sobriquets like Manure, Vile or Cheatski and none of the ridiculous hyperbole or metaphors to depict just how much we hate Ferguson, Rooney, Drogba et al. This is to be an essay on the prospects of a successful England football campaign in the southern most state of the African continent that is to transpire in June and July of this year and, extrapolating the hypothesis further, a corollary to explain the likely success or otherwise of our national football team in any future major tournaments. Confused? More likely, you're switched off already. And, with that, I rest the case that I am about to present.

The reason we love and live football is because it is our opportunity to not follow convention or logic. It gives us the chance to make outra-

geous, indefensible statements and to make idiots of ourselves in front of a TV screen or other adults when Everton score or the referee makes a decision that we don't agree with. Football for us is raw emotion. Take out the emotion and it becomes pointless. That is why true Evertonians do not actually give a fig for the prospects of the England team and find international weekends an interminable bore. The problem for us, you see, is we Evertonians are passionate. On the other hand, once a player pulls on the Three Lions, their passion dissolves. Playing football becomes a mere job, a duty, a chore even. That is why Evertonians, by and large, are not interested in our national team. More significantly, that is the reason that England will probably falter somewhere between the group stages and semi-finals in South Africa this year, and probably on penalties.

And why are England and their fans once again being taken in by the hype of a foreigner in the Emperor's Clothes, who is going to get the team no further than the quarter-finals of a World Cup before buggering off with a shed full of compensation as the newspapers slaughter him and then slaughter the whole nation for being stupid enough for actually believing that England were good enough to beat the world at football? And those beer-stained fat bellies will attempt to smash up the bars in Nelson Mandela Bay and then wish they hadn't when they discover 'sensitive policing' is not a term familiar in this part of the world. It is a scenario that is almost as crystal clear as if it had already happened. It hasn't actually taken place yet, but, trust me, it will.

We are now entering a year that has been anticipated with almost unbearable anticipation on this continent since 15 May, 2004 when the decision was made to host the World Cup on African soil for the first time since football was invented. It is so ingrained on the psyche of every inhabitant of this vast continent, that when I was explaining to my 6-year-old daughter on 31 December that tomorrow will be 2010, she immediately responded with: "You mean, twenty ten, FIFA World Cup?" I have to say, I am also extremely excited. I can remember barely a detail of the last World Cup and, let's face it, the final was instantly forgettable and this has been a trend over the past two decades. Perhaps, partly because I have seen the final in ever-increasing states of inebriation over that time, but more, I think, because the football played has become increasingly sterile with teams cancelling each other out as coaches' tactics become ever more sophisticated and dependent on avoiding defeat rather than actually trying to win the game. Some naïve optimism is telling me, though, that the change of air and scenery offered by Cape Town, Johannesburg and the like is going to lift this World Cup to new heights. Maybe the entertaining and erratic African teams can prevail on their own patch, bringing a dimension of unpredictability that has been sadly lacking in international football for a very long time. Personally, I would love to see Joseph Yobo lift the Jules Rimet trophy. Corrupt and brutal as the Nigerian nation might be, it would add real spice to the year and it's the only chance we have of seeing an Evertonian captaining a World Cup winning team. Sadly, his country's form has aligned itself pretty much with our own dear Joey, so the chances of The Super Eagles flying to the top of the tree are, well, to be frank, about the same as those for England.

Despite all this optimism for the tournament, why can I still not raise even a flicker of interest in the prospects of England? It wasn't always like this. In 1986 I was as angry and devastated as most of the nation was when Maradona cheated us out of Mexico in the quarter-finals. Not quite as heartbroken as when Everton had finished second to Liverpool in the league and F.A. Cup two months earlier, but upset nonetheless. My first experience of true football desolation was when England threw away a two goal lead to lose to West Germany, again in a Mexico quarter-final, sixteen years earlier. It was in 1998, though, when I can truly identify the first World Cup in which I was indifferent to the success or otherwise of my fellow nationals. In fact, indifferent is being too kind; I positively revelled in the moment that Beckham was sent off and, thus contributed to the elimination of England at the hands of the Argies.

So, what happened between 1986 and 1998? Perhaps the clue comes in the year that bisects those two. 1992 was the year of the birth of the

Premier League. There is no doubt it was a marketing masterstroke. With a new name and a reduced elite number of teams (eventually), suddenly people who had turned their back on football amidst the hooliganism, cynicism and negative football of the 70s and 80s, came rushing back. Miraculously, due to some magical rebranding and some extra dosh, grounds like Goodison Park were filled with 35,000 every week by the mid-nineties to watch, let's be honest here, pretty mediocre fare, whereas a decade earlier we could barely muster 28,000 on a regular basis to see probably the best team in Europe. I never fully understood it, but I definitely recognised the value of marketing from that day forth. There was a much less savoury effect of that transformation, though, as it was the beginning of the widening of the divide between rich and poor. All-seater stadia and the accompanying price hike, obviously favoured the likes of Man Utd with their massive ground capacity, but also the prize money meant success bred success on an accelerated scale. The subsequent riches of the Champions League shared out to clubs that were, in general, far richer than everyone else anyway, all contributed to a chasm being formed in the English top flight that, apart from ourselves in 2005, has hardly been crossed in this millennium. The megalomaniacs from Russia, America and the Middle East have got a whiff of the money and the associated glamour and have added to the 'haves' having even more or allowing the likes of Money City to sneak in to the select league by default. Given that I don't want Everton to become one of these 'elite clubs' by such 'non-football' means (and I suspect Bill Kenwright is the same!) the only hope for people like Bill and me, is that the divide is removed by the excellence of Moyes adding enough value to Everton's performances to surpass the underachievement of others that is an inevitable consequence of employing incompetents like Hughes or Benitez (and, increasingly, Sir Alex Ferguson) at their helm. The overall product may have improved, but the sense of fair competition diminished as soon as huge amounts of money were thrown at the top league in English football. Some clubs did a 'Dubai' and pretended they could live beyond their means and came to a pretty sticky end, such as Southampton and Leeds. Others now stand on the precipice, like West Ham and Portsmouth, while Everton remained prudent but uninspiring. And much of this distribution of riches came down to timing. If the Premier League had arrived in 1985, Everton would have hit the ground running and, who knows what might have happened? Whereas Man Utd were perennial mid-table anonymity at that time. Fortunately, by 1992, Liverpool had already started to implode under Graeme Souness. Imagine Liverpool being about to win their 30th title now? It's a sobering but, ultimately heart-warming thought, to know we were probably about two years away from that happening!

The other aspect that came with the Premier League and its untold fortune was the influx of foreign players. Attracted by the Premier League's image, they began to flock in. But was it really the exciting style of football or was it the exciting size of the pay cheque? Probably the latter, and that is when the self-centred, money-obsessed professional footballer was born. For me, it was when my interest in the national team died. The England team is made up almost exclusively of players with this mentality. Lescott will no doubt become a regular in the international set-up since moving to Money City and he is typical of the type that pulls on the England shirt. You name a single player in Capello's squad who you could associate with the word loyalty (apart from possibly Terry and Gerrard, although they have both had their wobbles and, I suspect Gerrard will be away from Anfield at the end of the season). Otherwise, try to think of a major England player who has not, at some stage in his career, moved to another club 'just for the money'. There aren't many. And that is why they consistently underperform for their country and why they will continue to do so and, therefore, why England will not win this World Cup or any other competition for that matter. They are professional in the sense that they do a job and get paid for it, but they are not passionate. As a fan, I have detected that and have become equally unmoved whether England win or lose. Compare the England players with some of the Evertonians playing in this summer's World Cup. Can you imagine Tim Cahill representing Australia without his heart on his sleeve? Can you imagine the same of Tim Howard or Joseph Yobo or Steven Pienaar? They play for their country with the same passion that they do when they represent their club. No club versus country conflict there, no half-hearted playing for the money, no bottling a penalty shoot-out. Perhaps that's the nature of the kind of players we attract at Everton and it's not just the work ethic and motivational skills of Moyes at play here. Is it a coincidence that the last time I truly supported England, the first eleven contained Trevor Steven, Peter Reid, Gary Stevens and Gary Lineker? Would those types of players ever be in the England team now? Maybe Lineker would, simply because prolific goalscorers are like gold dust and he wasn't with us long enough to be a True Blue, anyway. But honest, down to earth, passionate players like Reid, Steven and Stevens? I doubt it. The world has changed since the advent of the Premier League and the players probably reflect society; less passionate, more antiseptic, choked by regulation and health and safety and the fixation with cash and celebrity. How glad I am that Everton as a club and, in its players, still has some of the old-fashioned values. Who knows, on 12 June in Rustenburg, two passionate Evertonians by the names of Donovan and Howard may assist in overcoming the robots of England. A triumph of passion over professionalism. I, for one, will not be at all sad if that happens."

And it nearly came to pass. England were somewhat fortunate to escape with a 1–1 draw against the USA in their opening game of the 2010 World Cup. And, apart from the prediction of Gerrard's anticipated move from Anfield, this article was fairly prophetic on many levels.

Chapter 26: To Hull and back.

(AUGUST 2010).

Everton's miraculous second half of the 2009–2010 season made even Sir Alex Ferguson consider us as dark horses for a top four finish in 2011. And the sensational run of form had all begun from a second half performance at The KC Stadium on a cold November evening in 2009, when we finally showed some fight against relegation certainties, Hull City.

"Well, what a season! I'm preparing to watch Fulham in the Europa League Final and then, at the weekend I'll be praying, like all good football fans, that Portsmouth can prolong this curious year of football by overturning the despicable Chelsea on the Wembley Farm. The season 2009–2010 will go down as one to remember for many reasons. For Everton, it really could be the turning point. I know, I've been saying this for the last six years, but I think the time has finally come. And I'm not just jumping on the bandwagon based on the last six months. No, way back in late November 2009 I was predicting this. On 25th of that month we produced one of the worst 45 minutes in David Moyes' reign. By half-time we were 3–0 down at the Kingston Communications Stadium to a team that, even then, looked like relegation bankers, and we were actually lucky to have nil! We scrambled it back to 3–2 but the ignominy was already complete, humiliation beyond recall; Evertonians hung their heads in shame in workplaces and homes around the world for the remainder of the week. Losing is bad enough but conceding the game before half-time against a team that hadn't beaten anyone of note for over a year? This was unforgivable, this was as low as it gets, I'm not sure about Hull, this was, undoubtedly, Hell.

Four days later we somehow rallied and pieced together a face saving performance against Liverpool but, incredibly, contrived to lose 2–0 at Goodison. So the writing really was on the wall. Which way would we go? Just three points above the relegation zone; survival seemed the target, not revival. Ever the optimist, though, I probably caused the *SFTH* editor more concern for my mental equilibrium, than a reason for optimism when I emailed him the following missive on Tuesday, 1st December 2009:

Dear Mark,

I'm trying to seek solace from Sunday's terrible results for English football: The RS beating Everton and Cheatski beating Arsenal. It's frustrating when there are so few Evertonians here and Violet is out on a week's expedition to climb Mount Elgon. I can share my frustration with my son, Chris, but he needs emotional support from me, not anger, as miraculously a whole load of RS fans have suddenly appeared from nowhere at school. As a father, should I really have inflicted this torment on my own child!? The performance on Sunday was encouraging, though, and I started doing some maths. Forget about Cheatski and Manure (and probably Arsenal) but, otherwise, the fourth place is there for anyone. I reckon, the way it's going, 65 points will be enough. That means we need 50 points from the remaining 24 games. Assuming we get nothing at Cheatski and Arsenal, that leaves 50 points from 22 games. That's 14 wins and eight draws. I reckon, if we play the rest of the season like Sunday, that is achievable. So, this Sunday is really a fourth place play-off (first leg) against Spurs. Everyone has written us off talking of relegation more than Champions League. Now work out where the 14 wins and 8 draws will come from and tick them off match by match. I hope Moyes is doing something similar. What do you reckon? You can put this as a letter in the next issue if you want, although things may have changed drastically by then rendering it all immaterial. That's why I wrote to you now because I knew, if I made this into an article, it would be out of date by the time it was printed. CLIFF.

I won't reprint Mark's response but, needless to say, he thought I was being ever so slightly optimistic. The rest of you might be saying; "well, we didn't get fourth place and we didn't get those 50 points so what's the big deal?" That's true, I concede. But, if you can recall how you felt after the defeat at home to Liverpool which left us behind Wigan, Hull and Burnley in the table and facing Spurs and Chelsea in the next two games with a whole back four injured, could you really envisage 46 points from the remainder of the season? Could you really expect just two league defeats in the next six months? Could you really believe the top eight for the remainder of the season would read:

1ˢᵗ MAN UTD 54 PTS.

2ᴺᴰ CHELSEA 50PTS.

3ᴿᴰ ARSENAL 47PTS.

4ᵀᴴ EVERTON 46PTS.

5ᵀᴴ SPURS 44PTS.

6ᵀᴴ MONEY CITY 42PTS.

7ᵀᴴ VILLA 41PTS.

8ᵀᴴ LIVERPOOL 40PTS.

You may say that this is distorted depending on which particular opposition each team played twice in these 24 games. Well, amongst our five repeated fixtures, we played three of the eventual top five, home and away (Spurs, Chelsea and Man City).

If we delve a bit deeper, we can embellish this with even more reasons to be cheerful. The first four games of this sequence ended in draws, against Spurs, Chelsea, Birmingham and Sunderland. If we calculate the league table from the Burnley game on 28 December onwards (i.e. the final 20 games of the season), Everton come third above Arsenal and just one point behind Chelsea. For the whole of this period, we were without at least one of Fellaini, Arteta and Jagielka, arguably three of our most influential outfield players. The points thrown away in draws against Arsenal, Birmingham, Villa and West Ham, not to mention the point tossed away by Donovan's unbelievable miss at Spurs, outnumber the points gained from slightly fluky last minute wins against Blackburn, Fulham and Pompey. We deservedly beat Man Utd and Chelsea and should have beaten the other member of the top three. We kept Money City out of the Champions League by playing them off the park at Goodison and out-manoeuvring and out-thinking them on their own ground. We gained more points against the 'big three' (isn't it a relief to no longer have to refer to the 'big four') than Spurs or Liverpool and the same as Villa. OK, so we lost 6–1 at home to Arsenal on the first day of the season but that was with the 'Elephant Man factor'. What excuse did Villa have for letting in seven at Chelsea?

There may have been a lot of 'what ifs' and 'yeah, buts' in the last half of the season. What if we had just managed a second half equaliser at Anfield, we would have finished in the final Europa League place ahead of Liverpool and what if Jagielka's header had counted at Stoke or one of the countless chances at Wolves gone in. Yeah but, we were lucky that Mido missed the penalty at Goodison and that Portsmouth had a legitimate goal wiped out on the last day of the season. In other words, in the world of swings and roundabouts we had a fair ride. eighth is what we got and eighth is what we deserved. 61 points got us into the Champions League in 2005; it wasn't even enough for the Mickey Mouse version in 2010. Even the 65 points I was banking on in early December would have not qualified us for The Promised Land. The fact that the top three would lose so many more games than they normally do thus distributing the points more evenly throughout the new 'big eight' was something that could not have been foreseen at the outset of the coldest UK winter for 30 years.

We have a 'New Politics' in the UK with Clegg gatecrashing the higher echelons of government. Is now the time for a 'New Football' with Everton doing the same to the Premier League? The statistics of the latter part of last season back up the theory. Two good signings, no significant departures and an empty treatment room would do it. Trust me, I know what I'm saying!"

From such optimism you could almost hear the crash of shattering dreams as the season kicked off. And, in terms of broken promises, Everton and Moyes outdid themselves on this occasion. No wins and bottom of the league at the end of September and not even a game against Hull on the horizon to target as the turning point.

Chapter 27: Murphy's Law.

(NOVEMBER 2010).

And here's a mathematical equation to explain why professional football is becoming more violent, or so the perception goes. Inspired by comments made by the person I strongly suspect to be the secret footballer.

"**Danny Murphy is a player who I have grudgingly admired. A subtle, creative midfielder tarnished by his wasted years at Anfield which, no doubt, also forged his suspect temperament. I always thought that he would have fitted into the Everton philosophy and style before he took that backward step from Crewe to Liverpool. We have a much better version now in Arteta, of course, but, before the arrival of our Spanish maestro, there was definitely a gap in the middle of Goodison waiting to be filled by a silky ball player of the Murphy ilk. He made a good move when he escaped the brainless bulldozer football of Liverpool to move, via Spurs, to the more sophisticated play of Fulham. Mark Hughes will, no doubt, wreck him with his absence of knowledge of what constitutes good football, but Murphy is approaching his football dotage now, so won't really care.**

Having shown a reluctant admiration for Murphy, I took more note of his recent comments about the psychology of some of the more thuggish teams and their managers than perhaps they deserved. Watching our matches against the likes of Stoke and Blackburn suggest that he was actually speaking the blindingly obvious when saying that these teams enter the pitch with an attitude of kick first and ask questions afterwards. Whether the managers of these teams actually psyche up the players into a frenzy before they leave the dressing room is, obviously, open to debate

and pretty much impossible to substantiate, but clearly the tackling seems to become more feral with every season from these lesser lights of the elite tier of English football. My intrigue in this topic was, not so much based on *whether* certain teams are becoming more physical year on year, but why?

Around the time of the Murphy debate we, of course, had the Rooney affair. Like all Evertonians, I just lapped it up. Once a Red always a Red, Rooney showed the kind of sensitivity and loyalty to Man Utd and their fans as he had done to us six years earlier. Somehow, this was so much more devastating, though. When he refused to stay with Everton, he may just have had a point when talking about wanting to win things and needing a club with ambition. Much as we, and most of the world, hate Man Utd, no one can say that they are a club that doesn't win things and isn't going to win more in the near future. We know that Rooney's brains are in his pants and he simply blindly mouths whatever Stretford tells him, in order to maximise his agent's income, but even I had thought that Shrek would have seen through his minder's cunning plan. Stretford is basically the surrogate father in this sad relationship and his 'son', without the benefit of a brain, does what he is told. Why is his agent suddenly so obsessed with manoeuvring a big deal for Spudface? Like a father, he knows his son better than anyone and he can probably see that his offspring's bad habits of alcohol, tobacco and sordid women are actually closer to addictions than the rest of us are aware. Seeing a George Best or Gazza scenario approaching, Stretford knows that this is the last chance for a big pay day before the downward spiral to the divorce courts, rehab and probably jail starts to accelerate. Apart from his unhealthy pastimes, which are already eroding his performances on the field, he also has a distinct lack of bottle, witnessed by the fact that he was harangued off the Goodison pitch by our fantastic fans two years ago, was totally anonymous in Man Utd's 3–1 defeat against us in February and was too scared to show his face in front of the Gwladys Street at all this season. As it turned out, this lack of bottle finally made him decide to sign on for another five years at the Theatre of Nightmares. When he saw the hordes of United morons massed at the end of his garden one night, he felt that, if he had any intentions of setting foot on a football pitch again without being lynched by supporters of Man Utd, he had better put his thumb print on the bottom of that piece of paper promising him a million pounds a month. The fact that he had already forced Ferguson and Gill to crawl to him like the disfigured beggars that crowd around the cars at every set of traffic lights here in Kampala, just added to the joy for the rest of us who inhabit the world of true football fans and genuine football stars (like Tim Cahill, for example).

So where is this all leading? Well, that Rooney statement when he slagged off the hand that fed him because it belonged to a club that lacked ambition, came on the day of the announcement of the blistering austerity cuts for the country. Ordinary people were suddenly fretting about whether they would receive any money at all on the very day that Rooney was demanding anything from £200,000 to £500,000 per week plus all the other add-ons. What is the raw emotion that this produces in virtually every normal thinking human being? Anger, perhaps, hatred, frustration, a desire to do something very unpleasant and painful to Rooney and his agent. I'm sure the tabloid stories of death threats were not exaggerated.

So returning to Murphy's statement. Why are players going out with fire in their bellies apparently determined to inflict harm on other professional players? Why does the crime rate of a country go up proportionally to the gap between the rich and the poor? As the rich get richer, the poor get more frustrated. The Premier League has become an increasingly uneven playing field over the past decade with the arrival of the likes of Abramovich and Sheikh Mansour bin Zayed al Nahyan, as well as the lopsided distribution of Champions League money. Teams like Blackburn, Stoke and Wolves know that they are not rich enough to compete. More money equals better players (unless, of course, Benitez is in charge of the purse strings). Better players equal better teams. It's still a sport, though, played by competitive sportsmen. Are players of these technically challenged teams going to simply accept that their team or they, as individuals, are not good enough and allow superior teams to trample on them? Of course not. What is the only way that they can bridge the gap?

Well, they can try to level the playing field by kicking the opposition. In a way, they are simply being realistic. West Brom and Burnley tried to play football in the Premier League and got buried. Stoke, Blackburn and Wolves have survived thus far with their more agricultural style of play. I'm not saying it is right; just like we can't condone the out of work guy on a sink estate who turns to mugging or burglary out of desperation, but it probably is one logical outcome, when money in the game, at the highest level, continues to make the competition unfair. And, just like the mugger doesn't particularly choose his victims, Karl Henry isn't geared to kick players from any particular team just to try to give Wolves a chance; he doesn't target only the rich. He'll assault anyone if it gives his team a little more chance of gaining three points.

The anomaly here, of course, is Nigel de Jong. He can't have an inferiority complex playing for Holland and Money City. I suppose, to continue the above analogy, he is like the banker or accountant, who is innately crooked and still wants to steal when he doesn't really need to. He is simply a dirty player who would continue fouling opponents even if he was playing in a Sunday league game against pub players. He is the sort of iniquitous character who breaks the normal rules of human behaviour that determine any law of economics. He is, perhaps, the exception to the universal football rule: $V=k$ $(R-P)$ where $V=level$ of violence on the field, $R=richest$ club in the league, $P=poorest$ club in the league and k is an arbitrary constant, let's call it 'the coefficient of aggression'. Quite what units are used to measure violence, I'm not sure. Maybe the number of potentially leg breaking tackles in a season. It certainly seems to go up every year, just as the gap between the richest and poorest clubs increases. QED.

So, de Jong breaks this rule that states that the level of violence on the field of play is directly proportional to the financial gap between the rich clubs and the poor clubs in that particular league. He is, in fact, the exception to Murphy's Law."

And then came Luis Suarez to further prove the theory that the lesser teams become ever more violent to compensate for their inadequacy.

Chapter 28: A Massive 'C' change.

(JANUARY 2011).

Finally hope was being replaced with despair especially after a humiliating 4–1 defeat at home to West Brom almost exactly one year to the day after that pivotal match at Hull. There's only so much heart deflating disappointment that this Evertonian could take. My emotional resources were threadbare... and then came Spurs.

"It was the great sage (or was he the great Brazilian soccer captain of the 80s?), Socrates, I believe, who mused that 'If you have a good wife, you'll become happy but, if you have a bad wife, you'll become a philosopher'. I think, if football had been invented way back in the time of this iconic Greek philosopher, then he would have applied the same postulation to football supporters. It's safe to say that when you support a good team, it makes you happy. Much as it galls us all, Man Utd fans are happy. They are also smug and nauseating but, it cannot be denied, that generally their lives are filled with a certain joyfulness. Chelsea fans were happy until about two months ago; now, on the whole, they don't exist. Money City fans don't know whether they are happy or sad as the jury is still out on whether Mancini's team is good or bad. Arsenal fans seem to live with a general disposition of bonhomie and so would we all, if we were treated to such eye-pleasing football every week. The second half of the theory also seems to work, though. If you meet fans of teams such as Wigan and West Ham, they do generally have a sense of realism and detached resignation to their fate whether it is to be surviving relegation or exploring the vagaries of the Championship. When you move deeper down the leagues, you find true philosophers. A Rochdale fanatic friend of mine takes a passing interest in the comings and goings of the Premier League but, no matter where in the world he happens to be, the first result he always seeks is that of the Dale. He was ecstatic with their first promotion in 41 years last season but accepts that it will probably be followed by their first relegation in 37. When you talk to him, he has a completely different perspective on the game. Winning brings him the exultation that we have all experienced (albeit only five times for Evertonians this season) but losing is an occupational hazard that he has become so hardened to, that it merely gnaws for a while before he accepts that 'there has to be as many losers as winners' and it just happens that Rochdale are not to be winners. A healthy dose of philosophy to rationalise the situation and make everything seem more bearable. This natural instinct for self-preservation transforms itself into a self-deprecating kind of gallows humour on occasions. Thus, when Rochdale led the League two table by 10 points with nine games to go and were staring promotion in the eyeballs for the first time in a generation, only to then pick up just four of the remaining 36 points on offer to limp over the line in third place, my friend said, "Only Dale could make a one horse race exciting."

And so to Everton. I am now wishing that I could inhabit the world of Rochdale fans; a place where expectations are lower than a Dachshund's dick. Where defeat visits as often as the postman, while victory appears at the doorstep about as readily as a plumber on a bank holiday. In that world, there is no crushing disappointment, no merciless barracking from colleagues and enemies; just the occasional innocent pleasure when, from time to time, your team happens to come off the pitch having scored more goals than the opposition. As an Evertonian, though, I was led to believe that this was our season. I really thought that we had filled in the final pieces of the jigsaw. Our defence was solid, our midfield creative and, we believed, our strikers were good enough. Form is temporary, class is permanent. Saha and Yakubu are class, we all convinced ourselves. Half way into the season, I now feel demoralised and humiliated. I can't look the Man Utd and Arsenal fans that swarm around me here in Uganda, in the eye. I no longer have a defence, I no longer have hope; my optimistic predictions at the start of the season are, quite frankly, embarrassing. I don't know where to hide. I am taking a crash course in philosophy to see if I can put some perspective into this desperate situation.

What really seals it for me, though, is the C word: CONFIDENCE. I'm not talking about the confidence of the players or the management, although, no doubt, theirs is taking a battering. No, I'm talking about the confidence of the fans. I have been so optimistic about my team and supportive of David Moyes, that I have usually avoided checking the Everton website after a defeat because I haven't wanted to read the negativity from a determined minority bent on crucifying the team and management at every opportunity. I accept that everyone has their own views. 'Football is all about opinions' as many a cliché-ridden critic has uttered, but I simply have preferred to avoid those calling for the demise of Bill Kenwright or the sacking of Moyes. Now, though, I have observed the balance has changed. My own mood seems to reflect that of a majority of the fans. The confidence of the support-ers has deserted them. They no longer believe that we are actually going to end up in a European place. In fact, like me, some seriously believe that relegation is a possibility. There has been a massive sea change, or should I say, C change, and the tide of positive feelings is continuing to recede rapidly. For me, the turning point was the West Brom debacle. Forget Beckford's profligacy, a team with any ambition of Europe at all, simply should not lose 4-1 at home to a newly promoted team who have survival as their main objective. It wasn't the result that pushed me over the edge, though. It was Moyes' comment after the match that did it for me when he said 'we were a bit flat'. Why? Whose fault is that? The one thing we could rely on with David Moyes and his team was that they would always be totally 'up for it.' For all their disappoint-ments under this manager, a majority of the players have always given 100%. Effort has never been lacking. Quality, maybe, but never sweat. When the manager concedes that his team is flat, it is surely the first sign that the manager's days are numbered. I desperately hope that

I am proved wrong. I like Moyes as a person, I like his candour and his commitment and I like what he has done over nine years at our club. In 2007, I wrote an article celebrating Moyes' first five years in charge, and said that he should be given at least ten years before we start deciding if he should stay or go. We are approaching the point of one year from that deadly deadline and, for the first time since he took over, I can honestly say that, in my opinion, progress is backwards and not forwards. A drastic change in mindset is now required to reverse the C change in the fans. Dare I say, a more exciting, risk-taking mind-set. Play two strikers, throw in some of the untried kids, give Yakubu or Saha an extended run or accept that they should be offloaded, one or the other but stop dithering, make game changing substitutions at half-time or even earlier if things are going wrong, not bring on Billy in the 92nd minute as happened at West Ham!

Something has to change and quickly or I might just have to set my sights lower and aim for a place that is more down to earth like Rochdale. A place where there is less distance to fall. As Socrates also said "He is richest who is content with the least." Was Socrates an Evertonian?

Postscript: I wrote this in the depths of despair after the Stoke game on New Year's Day. We have just had possibly our best 45 minutes of the season in the second half against Spurs. Supporting Everton really is like being married to an unpredictable woman; a roller coaster of emotions, from near divorce to passionate love in the space of a day. I still wouldn't mind a trophy, though, Dave!"

This article was written when my own future as leader of a large establishment was in the lap of the Gods. Indeed, I lasted as Head of Rainbow International School for almost exactly the same length of time that David Moyes managed Everton Football Club. We both resigned when we felt the time was right. The sell-by date for moderately successful Evertonian leaders appears to be around the 11 and a half year mark.

Chapter 29: Stumbling Block.

(AUGUST 2011).

Back in the UK and closer to the action, my mood remained somewhat fatalistic.

"I have kept away from football news this close season. Evertonians have learnt over the past three years since our last signing of note (Fellaini on deadline day 2008) that transfer news is something that happens to others. Hanging on to players that are already on our payroll is the closest that we come to a signing. How we sighed with relief when Arteta signed a four year deal and when Cahill extended his stay towards retirement age. Jagielka also gave us reasons to be cheerful although he has been the subject of Arsene's green eye ever since he agreed to stay at Goodison for another four years. At the time of writing we still don't know if he will be partnering Thomas Vermaelen at the Emirates come September.

There are two aspects to this frustrating state of affairs that torment Everton fans more than anything:

1. How is it that teams such as Stoke City, West Brom, Bolton and Fulham with average gates well below ours manage to acquire at least one exciting new signing every summer? And:

2. Why don't we at least pick up on some out of contract free transfers?

As it is, we are entering a new season exactly as we ended the last; with a strike force consisting of two players who do not have the technical ability for the Premier League, a classy crock and a former excellent finisher who has never fully recovered from an Achilles injury sustained 3 years ago. You can fill in the names. The rest of the team looks solid but, if you can't score goals, which we will not, you have no chance of finishing much above middle even with the miracle worker, Moyes in charge.

As I have said, I have kept away from football related literature this summer. That includes the Everton websites. This has been for fear of being depressed too much, but I can guess that Bill Kenwright has been taking a caning. I must admit, from the outside it is hard to understand why our financial position does appear to be so parlous. We are on the outside, though, and so it is difficult to make informed judgments without the full facts. Of course, better communication from the Board to the fans might alleviate some of the anguish and suspicion.

There was one statement that I caught from a snippet of sports news on Sky this week, though, that I thought summed up the wider problem that now afflicts football. While we were treated to views of the gangly Emmanuel Adebayor demonstrating his languid skills during a photo shoot at Real Madrid, the voiceover stated that the former Arsenal striker was set to join Spurs, although his current wages of £170,000 per week could be a stumbling block. The question that immediately flashed into my head was 'Why?' For the rest of this article, I am going to enter the world of normal people, the world of you and me, the world that means that there is no logical explanation as to why Adebayor will not sign for Tottenham. If it was due to some allegiance to his former mentor, Wenger, or more general pangs of loyalty to Arsenal as a whole, the club that, basically made him a much better player than he really is, then it may be understandable that he would not want to pull on the white shirt of Arsenal's bitterest rivals. However, we all saw his total disregard for the Arsenal fans and his disrespect for the Arsenal manager, when he gloated mercilessly after scoring for Money City in his first game against his former team mates two years ago. This action in itself shows the kind of character that he is and the kind of arrogant, greedy monster that the modern game has now created; the kind of self-obsessed egomaniac that thinks that earning less than £170,000 per week is somehow beneath him. In the real world, you and I can only dream of having a job where we might earn £170,000 per year, let alone a week; People who live in the real world know that, if they earned £170,000 per week, they would only need to work for six months in order to never have to work again for the rest of their lives. If you or I had a God given talent for football, we'd probably play for Everton for nothing for the rest of our career, after picking up our first six months' wages, just to help out our poor club's finances. But that's the point, we do not inhabit that world, we do not have that God given talent, so we do not know what it is that grips these individuals when they enter the world of top flight football. One thing that grips them, of course, is the blood stopping crush of an agent's hand. For many footballers, they have absolutely no other talent that extends beyond football. Their brains literally are in their boots and they are easy prey for the manipulative Mr ten per cent. Players like Adebayor, with no real affinity to any club, soon develop their devotion to the dosh. Money takes over. Adebayor would rather sit in the reserves or on the bench earning his fortune than do what he loved doing on the beaches of Togo as a kid, and actually play the game. If he had a brain, he would see that he could do both; even on £5000 a week, which is much more than most people in the real world earn, he could live a life of luxury and still play football every week for a club like... well, Everton.

Money City are trying to buy the league title and, sadly, I think they might succeed even with their fragmented playing style and negative mindset. The individual talent is so great that, even though the whole is much smaller than the sum of the parts, the parts might just produce enough sublimity to prevail. Having bought every superstar currently available, they now find themselves with a massive stock of expired goods. Just consider the strikers; Bellamy, Wrong-Phillips, Santa Cruz and, yes, our friend, Emmanuel. To other teams they have not reached their sell-by date. It's just that the Arabs have moved into a new stratosphere and these players are now considered not good enough for them or, more specifically, their capricious Italian manager.

These players need to be offloaded and quickly. It's a fire sale and the proceeds do not have to be significant. Half price, 70% off, buy one, get one free; I'm sure the Sheikhs are flexible. So why are these players still collecting cobwebs in the Carrington corridors? This is why; it is because of that previously referred to stumbling block. Short Wrong-Phillips who has made more disastrous career moves than most, would still rather warm the bench at The Etihad than further his flagging England chances with regular football elsewhere. Santa Cruz will continue getting splinters in his arse rather than try to recreate his fantastic first season in English football and Bellamy, well he's just a nasty knobhead who would sell his own grandmother for a few readies. Even when he went to help his boyhood club *not* get promotion from the Championship last season, he did it on Premier League wages paid by the stupid oil merchants. The reason why these idle stars are remaining idle is because of this immovable stumbling block. They have not done the sums that would tell them that in the real world £170,000 is a mortgage that will hang around the average person's neck for 25 years, not something you pick up in a weekly wage packet. They also have not realised how angry and, dare I say, jealous that has made the man on the street who actually pays the salaries of these prima-donnas by parting with upwards of £30 to watch the team each week; a team without them even in it. When Rio Ferdinand tweeted his appeal to those on council estates not to riot because, as he bragged, he had also once been like them but now was obscenely rich, didn't he realise how that would simply wrench up the ante? If ever there was an incitement to cause civil unrest, that was surely it.

As an Evertonian, didn't you want us to sign Wrong-Phillips or even Santa Cruz? At least we'd have someone with pace or a striker with a first touch better than a giraffe. No doubt, we could get them at a knock down price especially with the new financial fair play rules about to come in to challenge the business models of the likes of Money City and Chelsea. But then we stub our toe on that stumbling block. Would

Moyes really break our rigid pay structure and, with it, our carefully nurtured team spirit, to bring in such a player? And could we afford it, even if he our manager did turn a blind eye to his principles? More significantly, would the player really accept a 60% pay cut? Of course not. That aforementioned stumbling block is an immovable object.

This article has still not answered the question as to why Everton seem to be completely hamstrung when it comes to spending any money but it does throw some light on why we perhaps don't enter the madness of signing a quality Money City or Chelsea reject. We still rely on the loyalty and reason of, what from the outside, appear to be decent human beings who have some sense of what the fans actually feel, the likes of Cahill, Baines, Jagielka, Saha, Neville, Howard and indeed, most of the rest of the Everton squad. Perhaps, that is why our new signings are so few and far between; trying to find such balanced characters in this money-obsessed profession is not easy. Given that Spanish football is now in meltdown as the central figures (the players) strike over the bankruptcy that they themselves caused, perhaps it is a warning to the English game. Players with this attitude threaten the future of the game and, therefore, their own livelihood. Players with the mentality that tells them that they should refuse to supply their product to the addicts (fans) who unwittingly provide their indulgent lifestyles because they are not willing to take even a token step towards the real world. Players who insist on their immoral salaries, and not a shekel less, whether they play or not. Players who don't give a damn about the people in the real world, the people who idolise them. An unrequited love of staggering proportions that appears to be ending in tears. Perhaps in this self-destructive selfishness, Evertonians can still hold their heads high and admire the view from their moral high ground that they still manage to occupy; intensely agonising as it may be. We need strikers but we don't need strikers, if you get what I mean!"

And ask any Tottenham fan of their opinion of Adebayor and his obscene wages now. There is no longer any such thing as 'value for money' as defined by people in the real world when it come to the world of professional football.

Chapter 30: In the School of Science, you should pay attention at the back.

(NOVEMBER 2011).

The end was nigh for *Speke from the Harbour,* with just four editions earmarked for what turned out to be its final season of publication. For me, this was the first full season of this millennium when I could watch The Blues first hand and I was already making observations that I may not have been able to make from my armchair in Kampala. Nothing beats 'being at the game'!

"In the 1960s Everton gained the moniker "The School of Science". The origin of this is not entirely clear but the meaning is. It was meant to portray our image as a team that played intelligent, sophisticated football. It is a nickname that we supporters of the club like to drag up every now and then to, well, console ourselves, I suppose. It gives us a feeling of some sort of misplaced superiority because it is clear that, when it comes to activities on the field, we are only superior to teams in the bottom half of the table. Our history is superior to all other clubs in terms of longevity in the top flight, but, in other ways, there would require a long discussion on the special definition of 'history' that we are referring to, when we try to tell a Man Utd fan that Everton's history is better than theirs. And, have you ever tried having a long conversation with a Man Utd fan? Not easy, is it? The words, monosyllabic and goldfish come to mind.

We are proud of our history; hence our theme song at matches and, it is true that pre-Premier League we could hold a candle up to almost any other club in terms of success. Only Liverpool had

really raced away from us in terms of silverware, largely because of the two decades immediately preceding the advent of the Premier League. 'The School of Science' comparison doesn't refer to trophies and victories, though. It is supposed to refer to a style of play. This is where Everton supporters can embarrass themselves. I mean, to what science were we referring, when Gordon Lee was in charge? Agricultural science perhaps. We had some great individuals in Andy King, Martin Dobson and, of course, Bob Latchford, but we hardly played it on the carpet. The same could be said of Joe Royle's curtailed reign. 'Dogs of war' is a far cry from 'The School of Science' unless we are referring to veterinary science, of course. What sort of science Walter Smith indulged in, goodness knows. Is there a Science of Sleep? I know there was a film by that title, although that was all about dreams. In the first half of the 1998–1999 season we just all dreamed of seeing a goal at Goodison, even from an away team. There were so many goalless draws, you could have studied for a degree in science on the Gwladys Street every Saturday; there would have been no distraction from the pitch.

And then we moved on to David Moyes' tenure. He is approaching his ten years in charge and it started with a bang. Once again, Woeful Wally had left us teetering on the edge of relegation and Moyes came in with a philosophy of, the best form of defence is attack. It was a little naïve in some ways as we were battered 6–2 at Newcastle but we outscored Derby in a 4–3 win at Pride Park in a crucial relegation battle. A massive contrast to most of what had been dished up for us in the previous decade. If we were to continue the scientific analogy, we seemed to be following a new course in Chemistry, with Moyes, as the mad professor in the lab, experimenting with explosive combinations and theories. With our Premier League existence secured for another season, things settled down after that. The gung-ho approach was replaced with a more considered game plan and we have generally gravitated towards the top half of the table as a result. It's been quite rare that "The School of Science" tag could be applied, though. Even when we finished in the top four, it was largely by default as Liverpool were so poor and our mass of single goal wins were often more athletic than aesthetic. When we replaced Gravesen with Arteta, we started to play more joined up football although, ironically, in that particular season, it was at the point that the mad Dane headed for Spain, that our form began to unravel. Since then, the presence of Arteta meant that the opportunity to play a more subtle, Arsenal type of game had been available to us, although not always used. When Pienaar was also in the side, we sometimes played some exquisite football befitting the term 'School of Science'. The 7-1 against Sunderland in 2007 and 3-1 against Man Utd in 2010 particularly come to mind. Those two players have now departed, though, and I question where our creative, thinking man's football will come from.

I returned to the UK in March this year after nearly 22 years living overseas. I managed to go to seven of our last eight matches at the tail end of last season. It was a mixed bag of results and performances. The win against Chelsea on the final day of the season was easily the best. This season, I've only managed to attend two matches, Liverpool and Man Utd at home. I have to say that I was very impressed with the performance against the latter, probably more impressed than with any of the other eight games I have been to since my return. Even allowing for the fact that Man Utd were licking their wounds and 'getting back to basics' after their humiliating mauling at home to Money City the week before, I felt that it was one of the best performances that we have put together in a home match against Ferguson's whingers. We matched them for possession and had far more attempts on goal. There is no point in harping on about the lack of a quality or confident striker to actually put the ball in the net; we all know that that has been a problem for several years now. The big change I noticed was that Tim Howard was not kicking long in that match. Even when we were chasing the game, which was the case for over three quarters of it, we still built from the back. Unfortunately, I only saw the 'Match of the Day' highlights of our match at Newcastle the following weekend, so I don't know if this policy was continued, but I hope that it is in future. By playing it short from the goalkeeper, possession is assured rather than entering the lottery of trying to win the first and then the second ball from a goalkeeper's hoof downfield. Brian Clough is arguably the greatest English manager of all time. His philosophy was very simple. He told his players to pass the ball to the nearest available player as often as possible. He managed the most over-achieving team in the history of football; turned a bunch of mediocre individuals into a Europe-conquering team. To him, possession was the raison d'etre of football and any player of even average ability could achieve it. If you were to write an instruction manual to a Martian on what the objective of the game of football is, you would say, 'for eleven players to try to transport the ball by use of their feet from one end of the field to the other and place it within the white rectangle at the other end of the field.' The Martian, assuming he is of superior intelligence as we believe him to be, would conclude that the players either move with the ball in their possession or pass it to each other. They probably wouldn't think that wellying it as far as possible upfield in the hope that a teammate latches onto it before an opponent intercepts, was the most sensible way of achieving our goal. It is not rocket science but it is the basis of 'The School of Science'. It requires the players at the back being confident enough to ask for the ball from Howard and for the midfield players to then be confident enough to collect the ball from the back four. It is up to the manager to instil that confidence and belief. I believe a professional earning over £30,000 per week should be expected to demonstrate such a modicum of ability and courage for his money.

So here's to the future, a future of neat passing football, meaningful possession and confidence with the ball at our feet, a throwback to Harvey, Kendall and Ball, a return to the silk of Sheedy, Steven, Bracewell and Reid. With the 'monetary apartheid' that the Premier League presently operates in, we are not likely to add to our history in terms of silverware, but, at least, we long suffering fans, can be entertained every week with a return to 'The School of Science'."

And there, the essence of Everton FC and the philosophy of its followers was touched upon. Six months later, as the curtain came down on *Speke from the Harbour,* I used its valedictory edition to expand further with an article that summed up what being an Evertonian really means and thus the title of this book was spawned.

Final Chapter: The Chosen Few.

(APRIL 2012).

"I returned to the UK a year ago after 22 years living overseas. When I left these shores in 1989 I had no great loathing of any football team apart from, of course, that bunch of Norwegians currently colonised by the Americans on the other side of Stanley Park. I've returned having experienced a massive transmogrification and I now despise many more things and people in this world than I did when I was the right side of 30. I am now the wrong side of 50 and, perhaps the natural aging process, has made me more curmudgeonly and less tolerant. A better knowledge and understanding of what is good has made me more aware of what is bad. Having experienced first-hand the less scrupulous people on this planet, I have developed the antenna to detect and detest from a far greater distance the human frailties of insincerity, negativity and self-aggrandisement. I have realised that honesty, integrity and humility are no longer 'cool', overrun by the more feral instincts of self-preservation, self-interest and a maniacal desire for instant fame and fortune. Apart from Liverpool FC, I now have an execration for most reality TV programmes, a majority of rap music, bureaucrats, fat cats and the health and safety culture with the salivating lawyers that it attracts. I hate racists, cheats, arrogance, spoilt kids and the debilitating obsession with obscene wealth that grips so many people. I also don't have much time for Balotelli, Tevez, Torres, Drogba, John Terry, Dalglish, Sir Alex Ferguson, Ashley Young, Rooney, Suarez, Chelsea, Money City or Man Utd. The more observant amongst you will discern that the last two lists were not entirely mutually exclusive. Indeed, they were two ways of cataloguing the same sad litany of what is wrong with this world.

Another reason that my objects of hate have multiplied in the past two decades from just the inhabitants of Anfield to a multitude of characters, characteristics and manifestations of the cesspool of human creation, is that, travelling to far flung parts of the world, I have found that I am occupying an increasingly smaller minority group in upholding my views of life, and football in particular. If you read Chapter 17 of my book *Expat Evertonian* (cheap plug) entitled 'How I came to hate United' you will see that the insidious manipulation of entire populations by the Man Utd and Liverpool arse licking TV stations, has helped turn the red of Manchester and Liverpool into global brands. Whilst I generally respected and enjoyed the company of many of my hosts in the various countries that I lived, I couldn't help but be irritated by the sheep like qualities they took on when it came to the Barclays Premier League. They bought the Liverpool and Man Utd hype hook, line and sinker. You could say that my frustration was borne out of jealousy; that my abhorrence of so many dusty bars on the impoverished streets of Kampala and Nairobi overflowing with crowing football fans clad in the rags of a second hand *AIG* or *Standard Chartered Bank* shirt bought from the local market with Rooney or Gerrard emblazoned between the shoulders, was entirely due to the fact that their teams kept winning (or, in the case of Liverpool, *used* to keep winning). However, I have a very reliable alibi here. It is called Arsenal Football Club. The success of the north London club has ensured that they also have a ubiquitous presence on this globe. But the crowing of their fans somehow did not grate like that of the followers of Man Utd, Liverpool and, latterly Chelsea (and, no doubt, since I left those places, Money City). There is something deeper to this than just the green-eyed monster.

Despite this monologue of gloom, I am actually a positive person. Ha ha; no, seriously. I am positive, because I honestly believe that I have been blessed to be an Evertonian. While so many tenets of human decency and pillars of estimable values have crumbled around me, as I make my way through life's fragile passage, the virtues of my football club have flowed through my veins like an elixir of life, the vision of Goodison Park standing there in my mind's eye like a temple of all things good. It might sound a little evangelical, but I am so grateful that I chose Everton as my club when I was 8 and a half years old. And such is the affinity I have had with Everton ever since, I am starting to believe that actually it was the other way round; I did not choose, rather I was chosen. Or, as the recent marketing literature from our wonderful club has suggested; WE ARE BORN, WE DO NOT CHOOSE.

Recent activities in the fish bowl of English football have reaffirmed my belief that the alignment of what I and Everton stand for is not simply a coincidence. I don't know quite what I saw in that simple royal blue shirt with white trim adorned by Joe Royle and Alan Ball when I first became drawn to the beautiful game, but there must have been a sign there somewhere. OK, so I was sniffing a scent of success but there were still plenty of other options. The success of Everton was very fleeting and none of my friends took the bait of a glistening league championship trophy in 1970, so why did I? The FA Cup holders were Manchester City. How did I know then that forty years on, they would become a symbol of the worst excesses of capital decadence. A team that pays its top player about £20 of each of his living minutes to play golf when he should have been playing football; and then to return from the other side of the world to mock his own fans with a goal celebration designed to emphasise just exactly what he had been doing for the previous six months and perhaps to thank the fans for paying for his luxurious lifestyle when they had misguidedly believed that they were paying for him to entertain them on the football field. City fans have lost all semblance of pride and self-respect, though. They don't even realise that Tevez and Balotelli are mercilessly taking the piss out of them, and they are not even going to receive the consolation for their blind, misplaced faith, of winning a trophy this year. Would Evertonians put up with such? I like to think not. This one wouldn't, that's for sure. At the dawn of the 70s Man Utd had a classy image with the likes of Stepney, Kidd, Law and Charlton. Perhaps the champagne lifestyle of George Best was a portent of how the club was to embrace the celebrity culture as much as sport in the coming decades, but it still had an air of respectability and integrity and was still basking in the afterglow of winning the European Cup as we entered the decade that fashion forgot. So, why didn't I choose Manchester United as my favoured team? How could I have possibly known at that time that all the virtuous qualities and proud history that the former Newton Heath represented, would be supplanted by a new form of gamesmanship, bullying of the authorities, manipulation of referees and the encouragement of cheating to achieve a winning formula under the pernicious reign of Sir Alex? Man Utd might win, but the cost is too great for my liking. Once again, I chose wisely. Chelsea were about to lift the FA Cup in 1970. The darlings of the Kings Road with their flamboyant skills and outrageous sideburns were about to outmanoeuvre gritty Leeds Utd in a replay. Pleasing on the eye (apart from the sideburns!), they would have been an easy team to latch onto. But I ignored them. Blue is the colour, football is the game, but it wasn't Chelsea's tune I danced to. And, once Mourinho entered Stamford Bridge to rewrite the philosophy of the club from fun to functional, from entertainment to defensive containment, from great games to mind games, Chelsea were never a club to be liked or trusted again. But at the age of eight, I had no idea what a rouble was, let alone that it would infest our national game with such grotesque results.

As you will read from the final chapter of my book, *Expat Evertonian* (did I mention that I had a book out?), one consequence of my time in East Africa was that I noted the infiltration of a strain of racism into the psyche of many expatriates that came to work there. Whether it was me becoming more sensitive to such tendencies, or whether there was a genuine invidious change in attitudes taking place, I cannot be sure, but I do know that I have become more and more intolerant of such attitudes as I have become older and wiser. At the time of leaving England, Everton were probably regarded as the most racist club in the country. We seemed to be the only club without a black player on its staff and there was a significant racist element amongst its following.

Regretfully I was acquiescent on the matter at the time. In hindsight it seems that, while the club appeared to be dragging its feet, it may actually have been taking a more considered approach to an issue that was, after all, not just confined to football grounds on a Saturday afternoon. Rather than jump on the frenzied bandwagon of condemnation with all its exaggerated handwringing and empty platitudes, history may show that Everton were simply taking a more dignified and intelligent stance. There was no quick fix and we were considering our approach to a sensitive issue. In the past two decades, I believe Everton's record on racism has been exemplary. Remember also we did have one of the first ever black players in top flight football in Cliff Marshall in 1975; a fact often overlooked when the racist accusations were flying in our direction a quarter of a century ago. So, while I may have turned a deaf ear to some of the moronic chanting and abuse aimed at black players in the 80s, I can now hold my head up high again in that respect. I can also be very grateful that I did not choose Liverpool Football Club to support all those years ago and, therefore, I do not have to try to explain away the spurious utterances and actions of Kenny Dalglish regarding his buck toothed striker.

How did I not end up supporting Arsenal? They were successors to our title in 1970 and coupled it with an FA Cup, as well. The following season, our inspirational and diminutive midfielder Alan Ball moved there. Perhaps, if I had been bitten by the football bug one year later, I may well have plumped for Arsenal instead of Everton. Perhaps it is fitting that the only member of my nuclear family to have strayed from the path of Evertonianism, has chosen Arsenal as his team, so there's a little remnant of my secret admiration for that club nestled within the bosom of our four walls. Perhaps it's appropriate that Mikel Arteta chose to replicate the journey of Alan Ball four decades on, after spending almost an identical length of time on the blue side of Merseyside. Similar sorts of players suited to similar sorts of clubs. Clubs with history and dignity, detached from the grubby world occupied by the other leading clubs with their moral vacuum and dubious values. Comparing the current managers, though, I would say there was still good reason for me to be chosen by Everton rather than Arsenal. Technically and tactically Wenger may be well ahead of David Moyes, but his selective vision and occasional submission to bouts of whining put him a few notches below our leader. Moyes' quiet, no nonsense handling of Royston Drenthe was such a contrast to the pathetic and very public U-turning of Mancini over Tevez (and probably Balotelli) or Ferguson's sucking up to Rooney's every little mood or whim. Drenthe is arguably our most gifted player but he is not bigger than the club or more important than our fabled team spirit. If it means less success, so be it. What a difference to the way Money City and Man Utd have kowtowed to their errant stars just to try to eke out better results. Mancini is just a weak man. Ferguson can't be described as weak. He is strong in the pursuance of results at all costs. A cost that includes allowing the likes of Rooney and Keane to sacrifice the club's past glorious reputation on the altar of unedifying personal gain. Would Moyes have publicly supported Suarez or Cole or Terry for their various misdemeanours? Would he have even allowed divers like Drogba or Ashley Young in his team? I think I know the answer and it is part of the reason that I am so proud to be an Evertonian. I wish for more success, but not at any cost.

And how are we chosen? Perhaps Evertonians are hand-picked for their honesty, humour and perspective; for their intelligence that allows them to understand the game in depth and to be able to suspend their excited anticipation of a semi-final to concentrate through a whole minute of silence in respect of a cause that may not directly affect them. An intelligence not afforded to all football fans it seems. (Supporters of Chelsea and Spurs take note). For their ability to not demand the head of the manager every time their club hits a bad run of results, for their intolerance of cheating and their recognition of honest endeavour. For their vision for the future and respect for the past.

Brian Labone said that one Evertonian is worth 20 Liverpool fans. I think his maths was wrong (the number is surely much higher) but the principle was correct. It explains why there are so many more Liverpool fans around the world. Like the hordes of Man Utd and Chelsea fans contaminating this planet, they have blindly followed. Evertonians, on the other hand, have been carefully selected and I am, oh so pleased, to be one of the chosen few!"

In the end, City did win the league, thanks, in no small part, to our good selves for grabbing a dramatic 4–4 draw at Old Trafford. One season on, City, like United, Chelsea and, of course, Everton, are all starting the 2013–2014 season with a new manager. It's a rare moment of instability at the top of the Premier League. Will the shifting sands finally provide an unexpected name on the Barclays Premier League trophy? Only when the ownership of these four clubs changes, not the managers, can we really dare to dream. What the hell; we'll dream anyway! That's what Evertonians do.

ND - #0096 - 270225 - C0 - 234/156/12 - PB - 9781780912318 - Gloss Lamination